God Working With God

God Working With God

Understanding God's
Reciprocal Nature as the
Greatest Key to True Intimacy

WARREN HUNTER

God Working With God is a trademark of Sword Ministries.

Destiny Image® Publishers, Inc.
P.O. Box 310
Shippensburg, PA 17257-0310

"Speaking to the Purposes of God for this Generation
and for the Generations to Come."

For Worldwide Distribution, Printed in the U.S.A.

ISBN 10: 0-7684-2400-3

ISBN 13: 978-0-7684-2400-3

This book and all other Destiny Image, Revival Press, MercyPlace, Fresh Bread, Destiny Image Fiction, and Treasure House books are available at Christian bookstores and distributors worldwide.

For a U.S. bookstore nearest you, call
1-800-722-6774.

For more information on foreign distributors, call
717-532-3040.

Or reach us on the Internet:
www.destinyimage.com

1 2 3 4 5 6 7 8 9 10 11 / 09 08 07 06

Endorsements

In this world, God has no hands but yours and no voice but yours. In Warren Hunter's book, *God Working With God*, he takes the power and simplicity of the Gospel and reveals the workings of God in us and through us.

—Evangelist Mike Francen
Francen World Outreach

One of the things I love about Warren Hunter's ministry is that it is not just an experience-oriented ministry. He is training us in the things of God and the glory of God, and in signs and wonders, and helping people understand the processes of God in their lives.

Warren Hunter is a Niagara Falls and he is like a 12-inch stream of blessing. He only has one mouth but he needs about 10 mouths for it all to come out. He explodes with what God has put in him. I love this man's spirit. I love what he represents. I love his passion; there's such an explosion in him.

—Dr. Mike Murdock
The Wisdom Center

I have known Warren Hunter since he was a child and have watched him grow up. Since a young age he traveled and did missions work with his grandfather, Bernard Hunter, whom I would consider one of the great missionaries of our time. I am continually impressed with Warren's knowledge of the Hebrew language and concepts. This man of God is full of the Word of God and has a unique revelation of the power of the Word. I recommend that you take time to read this book. I am convinced that it will bless you and draw you into greater intimacy with God.

—Dr. Terry Law
World Compassion Ministries

I have been friends with Warren for several years. I've always enjoyed his memory and revelation concerning the Word of God. I can see within his life, the evidence of how God is working in his life. I believe within this book you will discover how and why God deals with us.

—Dr. Gary Smalley
Author, *I Promise*

Contents

Introduction

ENCLOSED within the pages of this book, I sincerely believe that God has a powerful and life-changing revelation awaiting you. As a matter of fact, I have been told by several key spiritual leaders in America that what you are about to read is not only a powerful key to unlocking realms of the spirit, it is also, in reality, a spiritual law. Of course, this revelation did not come overnight. Several years ago I began ministering on the portrayal of God's glory in Scripture. In this teaching I began to see an incredible cycle that provided a glimpse into the very nature of God.

Beginning with the book entitled *Keys to a Yielded Will* and progressing through *Presenting a Yielded Will*, among other works, God was steadily unfolding to me a very special and progressive revelation. From there we went on to *From Fire to Glory*, a book that speaks of the supernatural experience of God working in our lives, a fire that is unquenchable and consuming, that human words cannot describe. In these teachings God was showing me an illuminating picture of His destiny at work inside His people. God's future is wrapped up in the covenantal relationship that He has with His church, and we must do our part to see God's kingdom come in full glory.

The revelation has never stopped developing. In *The Unlimited Realm*, volumes one and two, spiritual barriers that hindered the unlimited power, love, and glory of God from moving freely in our lives were broken. After that, both *Supply of the Spirit* and *The Glory of the Anointing* were birthed out of a clear revelation of the words of Paul in Colossians 1:27: *"Christ in you, the hope of glory,"* a blueprint that God has forever stamped on my heart. The message was then tempered with the revelation of the power of God's purity in the books entitled *Transparency* and *The Power of Innocence*.

Recently, however, God has been opening my eyes to a spiritual principle that is the culminating work of all the revelation that God has given me so far; this revelation connects virtually everything that the Spirit has taught me in ministry for over 18 years. This unfolding message is the result, not just of the above-mentioned books, but also of thousands of supernatural revival services that my wife and I have held all around the globe—meetings in which the power of the living Word and the revelatory principles that God has unveiled to me were more than evident. Though one might call this book by many titles (because the revelation is intertwined throughout the whole Bible and stretches from Genesis to Revelation, thousands of times), none explains this abiding truth better than the title *God Working With God*.

You are about to begin a brand-new spiritual journey. I believe, without a doubt, that what I am about to share with you will forever change the way you understand God and His mighty Word. It reaches into His Spirit, revealing His very nature and the complexities of the inner workings of His heart. I encourage you to dig deeply into this fresh revelation and find God's best and God's rest. Allow the Holy Spirit to enlighten you while you read and you will see that this profound truth is literally going to explode within your spirit, creating an imprint on your consciousness. In its simplicity you will be forever reminded of just how near God is.

CHAPTER ONE

To Be Believed

HOW BIG IS GOD?

ASK typical believers how big God is and you would probably not be surprised to find them ever ready to acknowledge the fact that God is all-powerful. Many would say it without even thinking. I have heard people say numerous times, "Sure! God can do anything. He's God!" But does His omnipotence show in their day-to-day lives? Is there any indication from their actions that they are genuinely aware of this truth? Are they walking in a place full of hope with their needs continually being met?

In the ultimate sense we know that God is unlimited, but from our everyday perspective, that is not always the case. Our perception can shrink God to an obscure idea that is smaller than the circumstances of our life. We tend to judge God and His Word by what we see with our eyes, instead of letting what we see with our eyes be judged and changed by God and His Word. As far as it matters to us, God can never be any bigger than our comprehension of Him.

Our individual revelation of the *bigness* of God establishes the groundwork for our belief. For example, if my picture of God excludes signs and wonders, healings and miracles, then it is most likely that I will never experience any of these things.

Your concept of God determines your miracle.

How big do you believe God is? Do you believe He is omnipotent? Do you believe that it is in Him that you live, move, and have your being? Do you believe that out of your belly flows rivers of living water? For the magnificent nature of God to manifest in your life, you must believe it! Remember all things are possible to him who believes. Scripture proves this.

> So Jesus answered and said to them, "Have faith in God. For assuredly, I say to you, whoever says to this mountain, 'Be removed and be cast into the sea,' and does not doubt in his heart, **but believes that those things he says will be done**, he will have whatever he says" (Mark 11:22-23).

> So He asked his father, "How long has this been happening to him?" And he said, "From childhood. And often he has thrown him both into the fire and into the water to destroy him. But if You can do anything, have compassion on us and help us." Jesus said to him, **"If you can believe, all things are possible to him who believes"** (Mark 9:21-23).

*For who, having heard, rebelled? Indeed, was it not all who came out of Egypt, led by Moses? Now with whom was He angry forty years? Was it not with those who sinned, whose corpses fell in the wilderness? And to whom did He swear that they would not enter His rest, but to those who did not obey? So we see that they could not enter in **because of unbelief*** (Hebrews 3:16-19).

Let me reiterate:
The revelation you have of the bigness of God
determines the groundwork for your belief.

Those who approach God must believe that He is, correct? The writer of Hebrews is making a simple yet profound assertion:

*But without faith it is impossible to please Him, for he who comes to God must believe that **He is**, and that He is a rewarder of those who diligently seek Him* (Hebrews 11:6).

Our ability to "come to God" is affected by our concept of Him. He is all-powerful, but if we neither see that nor believe that of Him, He will never be all-powerful toward us or in us. *We are hindered from entering into the fullness of the revelation He has for us because of unbelief.* Furthermore, if we fail to recognize that He is a rewarder of those who diligently seek Him, how can we hope for a reward?

Before the Lord can effectively act on our behalf, we have to progressively pursue a walk of trust with Him. The world often repeats the message, "Trust no one but yourself." This kind of thinking saturates our society in songs, television, and popular philosophy. So how do we really convince ourselves to trust and believe in God? As humans, we are not born with this kind of trust, any more than we are born knowing how to read and write. Trust must be taught. What is more, we have to know exactly what it is that most effectively builds trust in God.

In addition to filling our minds continually with the truth regarding His nature and abilities, we need God's Word branded on our consciousness so that we will never forget how powerful His words are. Even the smallest child who grows up in Sunday school can recount how God parted the Red Sea and shut the mouths of the lions for Daniel—children know the acts of power that God has done. They must also be taught, however, that the actual words of God contain God's creating power. To know, believe, and receive His words is the key to being transformed into the image of His Son.

A phrase that Dr. Mike Murdock likes to use is, "What you respect, you will attract; what you don't respect, you will repel." When taken to heart this truth can open a door to a new attraction of God's power through knowledge and respect of God's Word. By developing respect for God's Word, we can expect His power to manifest in our lives. One could also say it this way: *To the degree that you value the Word, respect the Word, esteem the Word, and exalt the Word, to that degree that Word works in your life.*

There is clearly a distance between God and this world—a wall of separation. God would be the first to admit this. He is holy, set apart. Holiness is a concept that is foreign to many people, even those who sit in a church pew every week. In many churches, it is taught that holiness is an unattainable, mysterious part of God's nature that cannot be grasped by simple humans. This view is very unbiblical, however. God tells His people in both the Greek and Hebrew Scriptures to "be holy, for I am holy." God says, "I am holy. Therefore, I expect holiness from My children. I sow the seed of holiness in you through the blood of My Son. The more holy you are, the more like Me you will become, which opens the door for you to receive more of My holiness." It is a never-ending cycle of sowing and reaping.

God calls His people to be fully set apart unto Him. To demonstrate this through the Word, God chose the children of Israel to be His holy people, completely set apart to Himself. This idea that God called His people out of Egypt (i.e., bondage, slavery to the world's way of doing things) to come into the promised land and be a holy people, is one of the great revelations of the Hebrew Scripture. (You'll notice that I refrain from calling the first half of the Bible the "Old Testament" because this implies that it is something that has passed away and no longer useful.)

In the Hebrew Bible, God commanded the Israelites to set apart one day out of the week to recognize that God was really their source. This day was to be holy, set apart. On this day, there was to be no physical labor. Why this strange decree? What was God saying in this special command to Israel? God was providing Israel with a physical way to begin to understand Him—a hands-on (or hands-off) lesson in holiness. By dropping everything on this holy, set-apart day, they would have a weekly reminder that it was a holy, set-apart God who sustained them. As long as they conformed to the principles taught in His Word, the Israelites could be part of the destiny that God had for the earth. When they began to take His Word lightly, they were really taking *Him* lightly. How they handled His Word was the key.

THE WORD WAS GOD

The key to developing trust in any relationship lies in the words we speak. Almost all human characteristics and attributes can be described through words. Confidence, arrogance, fear, joy, understanding, wisdom, love, hatred, bitterness, worry, and peace are all traits or mind-sets of humans that can be understood through words. In relationships, others will judge us based on what we say. *Are the words that I say full of doubt and fear, or are they positive and uplifting? My true motives and the deep secrets of my heart will always be shown through the words that I choose.*

Likewise, a person's actions are linked to their words in a very important way. Trust is built between two people when what the partner speaks lines up with what he or she does. They will judge each other's character based on their consistency in making sure that what they speak comes to pass. This is an area where most people have been let down by others. From the earliest age, people experience the failure of authority figures to keep their word. From little things, such as a forgotten birthday, to the biggest ones, such as a father deserting his family, children are trained not to trust what others say.

Slowly, the importance of watching what we say and being truthful has been worn away by the so-called role models in our lives. Our society as a whole is filled with suspicious people who refuse to trust anyone. This is a big change for a country where, 100 years ago, verbal contracts were legal and binding and a common occurrence. And, when a person signed his name to a contract, this action meant that he was binding his ability to choose according to the agreement that he had already made. This is not so any longer. Now it is more a question of which legal loophole can be used to get out of a contract, so that person may be free to break his word whenever he feels like it. Have you ever heard the expression: "Talk is cheap"? By using this expression, people are really saying, "We must wait to see if someone's actions back up what they say." Normally, only time will tell.

So what is the point to all of this? Not surprisingly, this modern attack on the integrity of words has strongly affected our ability to trust God. Humans always judge God by their experiences with others. For instance, if a person had a horrible father who was never at home and did not take care of his family, this is the picture he will have in his head every time someone mentions that God is the Father. If the people around us, whom we have seen face to face and who claim to love us, do not keep their word to us, why should we believe that God, whom we have not seen, can do any better?

Do not be deceived. None of this is an accident. Our enemy, the devil, knows the power of words and their importance in God's eyes. The devil knows that all things were created by God's words; therefore, he is trying his best to stop us from believing what God says, so that we will never be transformed by His word. The devil's tactic is to plant seeds of doubt and confusion in our thoughts, to constantly bring up the past and our present circumstances in order to distract us from what God says about us. As a result of his work, many believers have become hesitant about fully grasping the truth of God's Word. The church has forgotten what David said in Psalm 138:2b: *"For You have magnified Your word above all Your name."* God has said that His Word is even more important to Him than His name! The children of God must be trained to open their hearts to God's Word and receive it.

Our relationship with other people should look similar to the relationship that we have with God. To grow in trust toward Him, we must spend intimate time with God, and watch Him perform His Word. If we choose to believe God's Word, we know that He is a rewarder of those who diligently seek Him. By spending time with God, meditating on His Word, our picture of the bigness of God will begin to grow, because we will see that all through the Bible God was faithful to do what He said He would do. We will learn that God is unable to lie. This is the first step toward taking God out of the box. However, we will have to lay aside years of doubt and mistrust created by the failures of the people around us. Our hearts must be restored to their original ability to receive words; receiving God's word as truth is the key to trusting in an invisible God. As Dr. Mike Murdock says, "God's greatest joy is to be believed. His greatest pain is to be doubted."

The Bible reveals its own believability from the very beginning. Honestly, that is exactly what it was designed to do. It quickly gets to the heart of the matter: It was written to be believed.

Jesus said in Mark 4:14 that the Word of God is like a seed. Like a seed of grain, it can be planted and has the potential to produce millions of seeds just like it—a whole harvest of mature plants. When God's Word is planted in a person's heart, it has the potential to grow and to produce after its own kind. We know that God and His Word are one—in fact God is the Word. When the Word of God is sown, God is being sown. When God is planted in our hearts, He has the ability to produce Himself—His own nature, character, and very essence—in us. That is why I explained earlier that satan always sows doubt and confusion in our thought life, bringing up the past and the present circumstances in our lives. Like Jesus said, satan is trying to choke the God-seed with weeds of doubt, confusion, the cares of this world, and the deceitfulness of riches (see Mark 4:16-19). He has been doing this from the beginning of time. Let us look at the story of man's fall.

In the Garden of Eden, satan came to the woman Eve and said, *"Has God indeed said, 'You shall not eat of every tree of the garden'?"* (Gen. 3:1).

Notice that satan questioned God's goodness. Satan did not ask about the tree of the knowledge of good and evil; rather, he asked if God was letting them eat from all the trees!

And the woman said to the serpent, "We may eat the fruit of the trees of the garden; but of the fruit of the tree which is in the midst of the garden, God has said, 'You shall not eat it, nor shall you touch it, lest you die.'" Then the serpent said to the woman, "You will not surely die. For God knows that in the day you eat of it your eyes will be opened, and you will be like God, knowing good and evil" (Genesis 3:2-5).

Again, notice that satan did not instruct Eve to eat the forbidden fruit. He did not say, "Come on, Eve. Why don't you just try it? Doesn't it look good?" Instead, satan twisted what God said, questioning God's word and His motives. He planted seeds of doubt in Eve's heart about who God is, whether God keeps His word, thus, questioning her very existence. Just as God works with the seed of His word to produce His own nature, satan works with the seed of himself to produce death and destruction.

❧❀❧

Grace is the avenue that God uses to plant His seeds.

Deception is the avenue that satan uses to plant his seeds.

❧❀❧

In the story of Adam and Eve, the weeds of doubt and confusion were able to choke the productivity of God's word in their heart; sin was born and man was separated from God.

Through grace we begin to see more clearly that God works with His Word and with His own nature and character. In this I discovered that God only works with Himself. God plants Himself within you so that He has something of Himself to work with. The Bible calls you the temple of the Holy Spirit. After you receive the Word of God for your life, the Holy Spirit comes and dwells in you and works with that word. God reveals more of Himself to you and then begins to reveal Himself through you, the outward manifestation of Himself coming from the depths of the Holy of Holies within you.

For example, we know from First John 4:8 that God is love. When we love God we are allowing God's nature to emanate through us to minister to God. In Exodus 29, verse 44, the Lord says, *"So I will consecrate the tabernacle of meeting and the altar. I will also consecrate both Aaron and his sons to **minister** to Me as priests."* When we worship God, we are ministering to God by letting His love flow through us back to Him. Clearly the Kingdom of God is within you and Christ in you is the hope of glory. The river of the fullness of who He is now flows out of your belly. No longer does the glory rest above the mercy seat in a temple built by hands; nor does the river flow out from the east gate of the Davidic temple. You are God's temple. You are the Holy of Holies. God has come to make His dwelling place in you.

The principle of God in Heaven working with God's nature and character in you is pervasive in the Holy Scripture. The greatest revelation of this principle has got to be in the cross of Jesus Christ. John 3:16 says, *"God so loved the world that He gave His only begotten Son...."* God loved us and longed to have a personal relationship with us. God sowed His son, (Emmanuel, God with us) the Word become flesh, so He could reap many sons and daughters. Through the blood of Jesus we can now draw near to God. God finished the redemptive work by fulfilling the covenant with Himself (according to John chapter 1, the Word and God are one), and now we can enter into the overflow of that covenant.

THE LAW OF RECIPROCITY

God began to reveal to me the spiritual law of God working with God many years ago. This truth encompasses the entirety of Scripture, so in reality there is no end to the revelation; rather it grows with every encounter of God's Word, as He opens my eyes to its unending possibilities. The first time I ministered on the portrayal of God's glory in Scripture, I began to see an incredible cycle that provides a glimpse into the very nature of God. The principle is woven intricately into the fabric of Jesus' teachings concerning the Kingdom of God in Matthew and Luke. In order to explain this amazing pattern of God's movement, which I call the *Law of Reciprocity*, let's look first at Matthew 6:33 (AMP):

> *But seek (aim at and strive after) first of all His kingdom and His righteousness (His way of doing and being right), and all these things taken together will be given you besides.*

If we understand that His Kingdom and righteousness is actually His way of doing things and being right, as the Amplified Version of this verse says, then we can gather from this verse that when we do things according to God's pattern of acting and being right, all we could ever need or want (all the things that the Gentiles seek after) will be given to us freely by our heavenly Father.

In His sermon in Luke 6:37-38, Jesus gives His disciples the following commandments:

Judge not, and you shall not be judged. Condemn not, and you shall not be condemned. Forgive, and you will be forgiven. Give, and it will be given to you: good measure, pressed down, shaken together, and running over will be put into your bosom. For with the same measure that you use, it will be measured back to you.

Here we have in Jesus' own words the Law of Reciprocity explained. Simply defined, the Law of Reciprocity is a mutual obligation or right. This spiritual principle is very similar to a physical law we all learned in school: For every action there is an equal and opposite reaction. We also see this law operating in our everyday lives. For instance, what happens if you smile at the clerk in the grocery store checkout line? More often than not, you will receive a smile in return—even if it is a half-hearted one! And is it not true, especially in the workplace, that whatever attitude you demonstrate to other people, those same people are apt to demonstrate back to you? It is true. What if you ask the person sitting next to you on the bus, "How are you doing today?" Will they not most likely ask you right back, "And how are you?" Yes, they will! What is it that we tell small children about dealing with others? "Treat people the way you want to be treated." When they do this, they have an expectation that they will be treated in the same manner.

Even though the Law of Reciprocity is so evident in our natural lives, somewhere along the way we have limited this law to merely external circumstances. We have not fully understood its spiritual relevance. We need to consider that God always follows His own elaborate design. If we see a principle demonstrated over and over in our lives, it would probably be a good idea to search the Scriptures and see if it isn't a law set into place by God to reveal Himself to us.

Jesus spells it out for us in the verses cited:

- Do not judge—you will not be judged.

- Do not condemn—you will not be condemned.

- Forgive others—you will be forgiven.

- Give—you will be given a superabundant measure, running over without end.

- With the same measure you use to bless others—it will be measured back to you.

For example, the biblical concept of giving can only correctly be understood through God working with God. John 3:16 says, "*For God so loved the world that He gave....*" It is clear that God gave His only Son as a seed because of love, the very essence of God's nature. When we sow monetary seed into the kingdom of God, it must be wrapped with the correct motive of love in order for God to reciprocate by His measure. God can only respond to what He sees of Himself in that seed (the Law of Reciprocity). If we sow out of bitterness, fear, or apathy, we cannot expect that God will have anything to answer. However, when we sow out of passion for the Father, God will be able to sow, not only monetary wealth into our lives, but more passion for Him. Jesus said, "*Give, and it will be given to you: good measure, pressed down, shaken together, and running over will be put into your bosom. For with the same measure that you use, it will be measured back to you*" (Luke 6:38). Give to God that He may give to you. When we honor God with our finances, we should expect God to honor us with His financial blessing (the Law of Reciprocity).

Honor is another attribute of God's character that we can fully tap into through God working with God. Jesus said, "*How can you believe, who receive honor from one another, and do not seek the honor that comes from the only God?*" (John 5:44). Jesus was reprimanding the people because the so-called honor that came from their peers was actually hindering them from believing (honoring) God and His

Word. Remember, no one can receive true honor unless it comes from God. Proverbs 15:33b says that humility always comes before honor. When we humble ourselves under the mighty hand of God, the Bible teaches that He will exalt us. Proverbs 29:23 says that only the humble will retain honor, therefore we know that humility before God, or honoring God above ourselves and others, is the key to receiving honor from God. Honor God and He will honor you!

This is the key to understanding why God answered Jabez's prayer in First Chronicles 4:9. The Bible says that Jabez was more honorable than all his brethren. When God looked at Jabez, He saw His own nature and character and answered Himself (the Law of Reciprocity). In other words, the reason God answered Jabez's prayer is because God found more of Himself in Jabez than anyone else. This clearly shows that *God is no respecter of persons but He is definitely of respecter of Himself.*

The Bible does not say that God wants us to put Him in remembrance of ourselves or our desires. Remember, God's Word is our contact with God. According to Isaiah 43 verse 26, God wants to be reminded of His covenant Word. A good example of this is in Exodus chapter 32. Here we see the Israelites rebel against God by making the golden calf, and Moses reminds God of His word concerning the Israelites:

> And the Lord said to Moses, "I have seen this people, and indeed it is a stiff-necked people! Now therefore, let Me alone, that My wrath may burn hot against them and I may consume them. And I will make of you a great nation." Then Moses pleaded with the Lord his God, and said: "Lord, Why does Your wrath burn hot against Your people whom You have brought out of the land of Egypt with great power And with a mighty hand? Why should the Egyptians speak, And say, 'He brought them out to harm them, to kill them in the mountains, and to consume them from the face of the earth'? Turn from Your fierce

wrath, and relent from this harm to Your People. **Remember Abraham, Isaac, and Israel, Your servants, To whom You swore by Your own self, and said to them, 'I will multiply your descendants as the stars of heaven; and all this land that I have spoken of I give to your descendants, and they shall inherit it forever.'"** *So the Lord relented from the harm which He said He would do to His people* (Exodus 32:9-14).

Moses reminded God of the promises He had spoken to Abraham, Isaac, and Jacob, and God chose not to destroy the children of Israel because of His Word. *There is no talent, gift, or ability that any human has that will impress God, because He is only impressed with Himself.* When we honor God and His Word, we can expect that He will honor us and that His Word will come to pass in our lives.

∽◇◇◇∽

Nothing impresses God like Himself.

∽◇◇◇∽

CONCLUSION: BELIEVE THAT HE IS

In conclusion, let us look at what we have covered so far. We understand from the Book of John, chapter 1, that God and His word are one. The Word is God. As Christians, we must train ourselves to believe what the Word of God says about the God we serve and about us as His children. What He has promised He will do, for God is not able to lie (see Heb. 6:18). When we accept the Word of

God, it becomes a seed of His nature and character that will grow in our lives and produce the very essence of who God is within us. Just as the Word of God became flesh in Mary's womb and the Son of God was born into the world, so God's Word can become flesh in us and make us into the sons and daughters of God that He has called us to be.

We also covered that God cannot work with anything outside of His nature and character. When He looks at us, He is searching for something of Himself within us that He can work with. When we love others, give unselfishly, and walk humbly before our God, we are offering to God His own nature and character. Because Christ in us is the hope of glory, we can have confidence that God is working with Himself within us to do and to will all that He has purposed for us to do.

Timeless Truths From Chapter One

- Your concept of God determines the groundwork for your belief.

  Your concept of God determines your miracle.

  We are hindered from entering into the fullness of the revelation He has for us because of unbelief.

  The revelation that you have of the bigness of God determines the groundwork of your belief.

- Grace is the avenue that God uses to plant His seeds.

Deception is the avenue that satan uses to plant his seeds.

- To the degree that you value the Word, respect the Word, esteem the Word, and exalt the Word, to that degree that Word works in your life.

- The Law of Reciprocity: "*Whatever a man sows, that he will also reap*" (Gal. 6:7).

  Give and it shall be given to you.

  Forgive and it will be forgiven you.

  God honors those who honor Him.

  Nothing impresses God like Himself.

CHAPTER TWO

In the Beginning

MEASURING GOD

LONG before Jesus Christ came to earth as a man, there was a God in Heaven who was revealing Himself in and among mankind. He was and is the God of Abraham, Isaac, and Jacob; He is the God who revealed Himself in the burning bush to Moses and through mighty signs and wonders in the wilderness. YHWH, or I AM, was and still is the God of the Jews. He is the Almighty Creator, and as Creator He is in a class by Himself.

As Moses proclaimed in Deuteronomy 10:17, "*The Lord [YHWH] your God is God of gods and Lord of lords, the great God, mighty and awesome, who shows no partiality nor takes a bribe.*" The Lord is an impartial Judge whose scales are right; His power and righteousness cannot be compared to any other. The Hebrew prophet Isaiah declared:

*Tell and bring forth your case; Yes, let them take counsel togeth-
er. Who has declared this from ancient time?...Have not I, the
Lord? And there is no other God besides Me, a just God and a
Savior; there is none besides Me. Look to Me, and be saved, all
you ends of the earth! For I am God, and there is no other*
(Isaiah 45:21-22).

Indeed, He is all in all, and it is absolutely essential that we catch
the revelation of God's uniqueness. Why is this an important starting place? It is because our concept of God determines our belief.

In the beginning God created the heavens and the earth
(Genesis 1:1).

The above statement comes from the very first chapter of the
first book of the Hebrew Scriptures. This book is called *Genesis*,
which is the English equivalent of the Hebrew word *bre'shyt*. This
Hebrew word also happens to be the first word in the Bible and it
literally means "source, generation, or beginning." This verse reveals
something very important about God in relationship to His creation
and to His Word. God is preeminent. God started start. Without
Him there is no heaven and no earth. This verse is our first impres-
sion of God. He is a creative God, and He is about to activate something that has never been activated before. As it pertains to mankind,
God is about to create man's surroundings, a place where he can walk
and talk and begin to establish a relationship with his Creator.

Now let us skip forward to another book that opens with those
same words. In this case it is the Gospel of John. Although the first
verse of Genesis shows us what was happening in the natural during
creation, the first verse of John shows us what was happening in the
spiritual during creation.

*In the beginning was the Word, and the Word was with God
and the Word was God* (John 1:1).

In the beginning was the Word. The vocabulary that John uses is very similar to the first sentence of Genesis, where Moses says, "In the beginning God created the heavens and the earth." Although we do not see the Word specifically mentioned in Genesis as being with God or being God Himself, we can see this principle demonstrated in God's actions in the next verses. Genesis 1:3 says that God commanded light to be, and light was. God commanded dry ground to appear, and it appeared. God sent forth His Word to create, and His Word created.

Commentator David H. Stern explains it thus:

God expressing Himself by commanding, calling, and creating are general themes throughout the entire Bible (the outworking of His justice and mercy shown toward the salvation of humanity). This expressing, this speaking, this "Word" is God; *a God who does not speak, a wordless God is no God. And a word that is not God accomplishes nothing.*[1]

The revelation of the power of God's Word does not stop at the end of the creation narrative, however. Throughout all of the Hebrew Scriptures, we encounter God speaking forth His words and bringing them to pass. Let us look at a few examples.

Then they cried to the Lord in their trouble, and He saved them from their distress. **He sent forth His word and healed them;** *He rescued them from the grave* (Psalm 107:19-20 NIV).

He makes peace in your borders, and fills you with the finest wheat. He sends out His command to the earth; His word runs very swiftly (Psalm 147:14-15).

The voice said, "Cry out!" And he said, "What shall I cry?" "All flesh is grass, and all its loveliness is like the flower of the field.

The grass withers, the flower fades, because the breath of the Lord blows upon it; surely the people are grass. The grass withers, the flower fades, but **the word of our God stands forever**" (Isaiah 40:6-8).

I have sworn by Myself; the word has gone out of My mouth in righteousness, and shall not return, that to Me every knee shall bow, every tongue shall take an oath (Isaiah 45:23).

A God who does not speak is no God at all.

The Word of God is not merely an indicator of His nature. Its meaning runs much deeper than any dim reflection. To describe God's Word as "powerful" is also too shallow a portrayal. God and His Word are one. That is why John says, "The Word was God." At the same time, unless God speaks the words, they hold no meaning at all. They are purposeless. Our God is a God who speaks to and through His people. The fact that He does speak, and everything He speaks comes to pass, shows that He puts something of Himself in every word that comes out of His mouth. Take note of this principle, because it is a key in understanding God working with God.

When God speaks, He puts something of Himself in every word.

God's words carry weight because the seed of His very nature and character is planted within His word. If this were not true, His words would be as pointless as the godless and unholy conversation we hear in the world every day. The Scriptures even say that God merely breathes and a new galaxy comes into place (see Ps. 33:6; Exod. 15:8; Job 4:9)! If one word from God sets the stars and moves the planets, just imagine how powerful God's word can be in our lives when we believe it and receive it. When we really accept that what God says is true, His words will first rearrange the way we think about things. When our old thinking patterns have been exchanged for God's way of thinking through the washing of the water by the word, we can begin to talk like God. Do you remember what Proverbs says about our thoughts?

Do not eat the bread of a miser, nor desire his delicacies; for as he thinks in his heart, so is he (Proverbs 23:6-7).

The Bible teaches that we are the prophet of our own life. For God's word to come to pass in our lives, God's word must be in our mouth.

Say to them, "As I live," says the Lord, "just as you have spoken in My hearing, so I will do to you" (Numbers 14:28).

To whom much is given, much is required.

When I first read this verse it shocked me. Immediately I thought that I needed to be careful about what words I speak. In essence what God was saying to the children of Israel was that in His eyes, their words were not "just words" as I have heard some people say today. No, their words carried weight with God. Because Israel was called to be a holy nation, set apart, a royal priesthood, a nation of ambassadors to the Gentiles, God expected that they would speak His words, not their own. When they failed to do this there were consequences. However, when they were obedient, there was the great blessing of seeing God's word come to pass. For this reason Joshua was able to tell the sun to stand still, and it actually happened! God heeded the voice of a man, because He recognized His own voice coming out of Joshua's mouth (see Josh. 1:8). If you want to succeed at causing the sun to stand still or moving a mountain, it is necessary to keep the truth of the Word of God in your mouth continually.

> *Then Joshua spoke to the Lord in the day when the Lord delivered up the Amorites before the children of Israel, and he said in the sight of Israel, "Sun stand still over Gibeon; and Moon, in the Valley of Ajalon." So the sun stood still, and the moon stopped, till the people had revenge upon their enemies. Is this not written in the Book of Jasher? So the sun stood still in the midst of heaven, and did not hasten to go down for about a whole day. And there has been no day like that, before it or after it, that the Lord heeded the voice of a man; for the Lord fought for Israel* (Joshua 10:12-14).

For God to respond positively to Joshua's command, there must have been the seed of God's own nature within Joshua's words—he must have been commanding the will of God to come to pass. Because Joshua's words were in alignment with God's perfect will, God heard and answered, and the sun stood still in the sky. God heard Himself in this command and brought it to pass. For more information on this subject, please read *GWWG: God in Your Mouth.*

For more information and for listening material on this subject, please visit our Website at swordministries.org.

THE SEED

In many ways, natural laws mimic spiritual principles. God set up the created world so we could look at it and see the God who created it. That is why God commanded Abraham to look at the stars; their vastness and beauty were and are symbolic of how massive God is.

In like manner, God created seedtime and harvest to mimic His own pattern of planting and harvesting. God designed His Word to operate in the same fashion as a corn seed. The farmer tills the land and prepares it with fertilizer so that it will be ready to receive seeds. Then he scatters the seed on the tilled ground, waters it, and allows it to grow. One corn seed planted correctly has the potential to produce hundreds of corn seeds that look, taste, and smell just like it. Therefore the farmer expects that in three months the plants will be ripe and he will have a harvest of corn. The farmer knows if he plants corn, he will not get barley or wheat. That's just impossible! Corn produces corn. Barley produces barley. Wheat produces wheat.

God's Word is the same! God's words are the seeds of change that are planted in our hearts designed to bring God a harvest. Here again we see the Law of Reciprocity (whatever a man sows, that he shall also reap)—when God sows His Word in us, He has an expectation that He will reap a harvest of His Word. In the writings of the prophet Isaiah, God puts it this way:

For as the rain comes down, and the snow from heaven, and do not return there, but water the earth, and make it bring forth and bud, that it may give seed to the sower and bread to the eater, so shall My word be that goes forth from My mouth; it shall not return to Me void, but it shall accomplish what I please, and it shall prosper in the thing for which I sent it (Isaiah 55:10-11).

In Isaiah 55, we see a picture of the Word coming down like rain and ultimately providing seed for the sower. It is not possible for God's Word to return to Him void because its failure would call God's integrity into question. Each word must accomplish its purpose. It will fulfill what it has been sent forth and designed to do because God is the Alpha and the Omega, the Beginning and the End. Just as He is the beginning of everything, He is also the One who brings all things to a completion. God sees the end of all of His promises. That is why Paul said, *"For all the promises of God in Him are Yes, and in Him Amen, to the glory of God through us"* (2 Cor. 1:20). God's Word is a seed, and God, like a good farmer, will watch carefully over His seed with the expectation of a great harvest (see Mark 4:14).

What is it then that this seed is designed to produce? As I mentioned earlier, every seed has a specific kind of plant it was created to yield. Apple seeds produce apples, corn kernels produce corn, and wheat produces wheat. What is God's Word designed to produce? That of course will depend on what the Word is. For example, Isaiah 53:5 says, *"But He was wounded for our transgressions, He was bruised for our iniquities; the chastisement for our peace was upon Him, and by His stripes we are healed."* If I believe and receive this Word from God, I can expect freedom from my sin and iniquity, perfect peace, and wholeness in my body. The question is not whether the Word is true. The question is, do I receive it as truth.

Another great example is in Psalm 91:

He who dwells in the secret place of the Most High shall abide under the shadow of the Almighty. I will say of the Lord, "He

is my refuge and my fortress; my God in Him I will trust."
Surely He shall deliver you from the snare of the fowler and
from the perilous pestilence. He shall cover you with His feath-
ers, and under His wings you shall take refuge: His truth shall
be your shield and buckler. ... For He shall give His angels
charge over you, to keep you in all your ways. In their hands
they shall bear you up, lest you dash your foot against a stone
(Psalm 91:1-4, 11-12).

This is an amazing promise of God's faithful protection of His children. Basically, He promises that if we will hide in Him, no evil will come near us. This should produce confidence in God and dispel all fear of the enemy's attacks. Healing and protection, however, are not the definitive goal; ultimately, all of God's words point to the nature of God Himself. In other words, healing and protection are not God's final aim; they are the fruit of the very nature of God Himself. Recall again John 1:1:

In the beginning was the Word, and the Word was with God,
and the Word was God.

I believe that the revelation of what God is saying about Himself in John 1:1 is the focal point through which we understand and observe all other truths. Because the Word is God, God is reproducing His divine nature in humans every time He plants the seed of His Word. Essentially, God is sowing Himself (God working with God).

Many times, Jesus uses the analogy of seed and harvest in His parables to demonstrate that God wants to sow His Word into us to produce a God-harvest. No single chapter bears out this truth as well as Mark chapter 4, in which Jesus instructs the multitude through the parable of the Sower. As you read this parable, pay close attention to what Jesus is emphasizing.

"Listen! Behold a sower went out to sow. And it happened, as he sowed, that some seed fell by the wayside; and the birds of the air came and devoured it. Some fell on stony ground, where it did not have much earth; and immediately it sprang up because it had no depth of earth. But when the sun was up it was scorched, and because it had no root it withered away. And some seed fell among thorns; and the thorns grew up and choked it, and it yielded no crop. But other seed fell on good ground and yielded a crop that sprang up, increased and produced: some thirtyfold, some sixty, and some a hundred." And He said to them, "He who has ears to hear, let him hear!" (Mark 4:3-9).

The key players in this parable are obviously the seed and the ground. We see from the story that not all of the seed that was sown produced a crop. Yet I doubt that anyone would say that it was the seed's fault. What hindered the crop from growing, according to Jesus, were not the shortcomings and mistakes of the seed; rather it was the failure of the ground to receive the seed sown. In the case of some seed, it fell where there was no tilled earth at all, and the birds came and ate it up. With other seed, we see that the earth was not deep enough to produce mature plants. These sprang up and died quickly. When the dirt was deep enough, the thorns choked the young plants and they died also. The seed was never the problem in any of these cases. Jesus made that clear to His disciples in His own explanation of the parable.

*And He said to them, "Do you not understand this parable? How then will you understand all the parables? **The sower sows the Word**. And these are the ones by the wayside where the Word is sown. When they hear, Satan comes immediately and takes away the Word that was sown in their hearts. These likewise are the ones sown on stony ground who, when they hear the Word immediately receive it with gladness; and they have no root in* *themselves, and so endure only for a time. Afterward, when tribulation or persecution arises for the Word's sake, immediately they stumble. Now these are the ones sown among thorns; they are the ones who hear the Word, and the cares of this world, the deceitfulness of riches, and the desires for other things entering in choke the Word, and it becomes unfruitful. But these are the ones sown on good ground, those who hear the Word, accept it, and bear fruit: some thirtyfold, some sixty, some a hundred"* (Mark 4:13-20).

According to Mark 4:14, the sower sows the Word of God. We know already from looking at John 1:1 that the Word is God. Can you see that God is really sowing Himself into the hearts of man through His Word? When a God-seed is planted in a person's heart it has the potential to produce an astounding harvest for God's kingdom! Once again we see that man's ability to believe and receive the Word can either hinder or help that God-seed to come to complete fruition. *"But these are the ones sown on good ground, **those who hear the Word, accept it, and bear fruit:** some thirtyfold, some sixty, some a hundred"* (Mark 4:20). A heart that is prepared and ready to receive is one that God is able to plant Himself in for a supernatural harvest.

Let me reiterate: God *only* works with God. That is how born-again believers can claim that they have received Jesus into their hearts. The Word of salvation was sown to the point where they could identify with the truth that it was really Jesus now at work on the inside to transform them into a "saved" individual. We say we have Jesus in our hearts; what that really means is that the sower sowed the Word, and it fell on good ground, producing God in our hearts.

In Genesis 1:2, the Scripture says that the Spirit hovered over the face of the deep. God spoke the word "Light!" and the Spirit of God went to work with the Word of God. Whenever the Spirit of God goes to work with the Word of God, creative power is released and something new is created. Isaiah 59:21 says:

"As for Me," says the Lord, "this is My covenant with them: My Spirit who is upon you, and My words which I have put in your mouth, shall not depart from your mouth, nor from the mouth of your descendants, nor from the mouth of your descendants' descendants," says the Lord, "from this time and forevermore."

The Word is in your mouth and the Spirit is upon it. God wants our mouths to be full of His Word so that when we speak He hears Himself and has something to work with. It is God's Word that has the power to create new things that have never been seen before. When the angel appeared to Mary in Luke chapter 1, he spoke the Word of God to her. In order for that Word to come to pass she had to receive it and believe it in her heart. She said to the angel, "Be it unto me according to your word." She received that Word of God, and immediately the Spirit went to work with the Word, causing a new thing to be birthed: the Word become flesh, Jesus Christ.

And the Word became flesh and dwelt among us, and we beheld His glory, the glory as of the only begotten of the Father, full of grace and truth (John 1:14).

Where did the Word of God become flesh? It was in a young lady's womb, correct? In Luke 1:45, Elizabeth prophesies over Mary, declaring, "***Blessed is she who believed,*** *for there will be a fulfillment of those things which were told her from the Lord.*" What if Mary had not believed? What if she had rejected the word that the angel brought to her from God? The seed of the Word could not have been planted in her to become flesh and display God's glory, full of grace and truth!

We need a God-seed or a God-word to be planted in our hearts. Only a God-seed or a God-word will produce a God-result.

God cannot work with our unholy emotions. No, God cannot work with our unsubmitted, rebellious flesh! God can only work with a God-spirit, a God-soul, and a God-body. Only when God works with God will we see the Word of God become flesh in our lives. Only then will we behold His glory full of grace and truth! That is why we must allow the God-seed to be planted in us so that God can produce the results that He desires for our lives. By creating a God-working-with-God relationship, where God in Heaven is working with God in you, God can work through you to be a sower of the God-seed, thus spreading His power and presence from person to person. This is the principle that God created to advance His Kingdom all over the earth.

Jesus explains this very idea:

And He said, "The kingdom of God is as if a man should scatter seed on the ground, and should sleep by night and rise by day, and the seed should sprout and grow, he himself does not know how. For the earth yields crops by itself: first the blade, then the head, after that the full grain in the head. But when the grain ripens, immediately he puts in the sickle, because the harvest has come" (Mark 4:26-29).

In this short parable found only in the Book of Mark, Jesus likens the Kingdom of God to the whole process of planting seeds and harvesting crops, very similar to the story of the Sower earlier in the same chapter. The difference between these two stories is their emphases. Unlike the first parable, here Jesus focuses on the sower. Even though it is a man who sows the seed, the sower remains in awe about the whole process. He recognizes that even though he scatters the seed, he has no ability to make that seed produce. God is the One who designed the system, and it is God who produces the results.

This is how God designed His Kingdom. He created man to be His partner in the God-destiny that He had already designed for the universe. As we scatter the seed of God's Word in people's hearts, He makes that seed produce His very nature and character, thus enforcing the victory won by God on the Cross and furthering the takeover of the natural world by His children.

In the beginning, God did not simply create laws by which all created things operate. He actually created the parameters or principles of God working with God, and by doing so, sovereignly bound Himself and His ability to act by moving according to those principles. These principles leave man responsible to receive God's Word before God can move on his behalf. This is clearly established in God's Word. For example in Deuteronomy, Moses tells the Israelites,

> *Behold, I set before you today a blessing and a curse: the blessing, if you obey the commandments of the Lord your God which I command you today; and the curse, if you do not obey the commandments of the Lord your God, but turn aside from the way which I command you today, to go after other gods which you have not known* (Deuteronomy 11:26-28).

God only blesses what He sees of Himself in us.

God was only able to bless the children of Israel if they observed to do all that the Lord had spoken to them through His servant Moses. God could only bless what He saw of Himself within the Jews, because God only blesses Himself. God can only deliver Himself! Why did God deliver Daniel from the lion's den? Well, why don't we ask Daniel?

> *And when he came to the den, he cried out with a lamenting voice to Daniel. The king spoke, saying to Daniel, "Daniel, servant of the living God, has your God, whom you serve continually, been able to deliver you from the lions?" Then Daniel said to the king, "O king, live forever! My God sent His angel and shut the lions' mouths, so that they have not hurt me,* **because I was found innocent before Him**; *and also, O king, I have done no wrong before you"* (Daniel 6:20-22).

We know that Daniel meditated on the Word, because this same chapter says he was skilled in the law of his God. Besides this, we know that he bowed before his window three times a day and worshiped and prayed to his God!

I can just imagine Daniel in the lion's den. As the lions circle him he cries out to God, "*O Lord my God, in You I put my trust; save me from all those who persecute me; and deliver me, lest they tear me like a lion, rending me in pieces, while there is none to deliver! Arise, O Lord, in your anger; lift Yourself up because of the rage of my enemies; rise up for me to the judgment You have commanded!*" (Ps. 7:1-2,6).

God, who runs to and fro over the face of the earth, looking for a heart like His, saw Daniel in the lion's den; God saw His Word, His law, His judgment, His own purity and innocence, and rescued Daniel from the mouths of the lions and from the hands of his enemies. I have seen this principle demonstrated time and again in revival meetings I have held. I now understand why some people could be ministered to and others could not. Even though they were in church and professed to be Christians, God was not seeing anything of Himself to work with in their hearts. He could not heal them, deliver them, or rescue them. He looked for Himself and found mere human beings.

GOD WORKING WITH GOD
THROUGH SEEDTIME AND HARVEST

Then God said, "Let the earth bring forth grass, the herb that yields seed, and the fruit tree that yields fruit according to its kind, whose seed is in itself, on the earth"; and it was so (Genesis 1:11).

Even the simplest plant shows how God desires us to understand Him! Each plant carries its own seed, holding within its power the ability to reproduce after its own kind. Within God lies the seed needed to transform all mankind into the image of the Father. The seed is His Word. God set up the natural system to reflect how He would send the seed of His Word to man. It was no accident. When God began again after the flood, He Himself prophesied that the system He created would continue as long as the planet exists:

While the earth remains, seedtime and harvest, cold and heat, winter and summer, and day and night shall not cease (Genesis 8:22).

Before sin entered the world—most religious people call this "The Fall"—nature was a perfect reflection of God's essence and character. Because of sin, God's enemy would now have access to the principles within nature that God had made to produce His glory. The laws of God working with God did not disappear from the earth; sin, however, opened the door, so that what had been good could now be used for corruption and perversion. Satan could now use the principles of seedtime and harvest to produce death and destruction. God had a plan from the very beginning, however, to restore creation to its original perfection.

Although the natural world experienced the corruption of death that came because of sin, that did not mean that God's promises and God's words were somehow null and void. There have been people in every generation who have declared nature to be evil, the body sinful, and anything pertaining to the goodness of God's creation to be humanistic. These people are forgetting what God saw in His creation when He created it. He said it was good! This God who knows everything, who knew man would fall into sin, destroying the purity and eternality of creation, smiled and saw that it was good. God saw well because He saw Himself, and He is still seeing Himself in creation today.

Paul said that nature is revealing God's glory to those who do not know Him, and David said the same thing in Psalm 19. God even told Abraham to meditate on the stars to learn about the bigness of who God really is. The amazing thing is this: God is actually working through us to restore all of creation to its original perfection.

As we walk out the principles of God working with God, we are enforcing the victory won for us and all of creation on the Cross, breaking the power of hell, sin, death, and the grave. Everything in the earth that was not planted by God will be uprooted, as it says in Matthew 15:13: "*Every plant which My heavenly Father has not planted will be uprooted.*" Unless God's hand was in it from the beginning, it was doomed for failure. The Psalmist says the same thing a different way:

Unless the Lord builds the house, they labor in vain who build it (Psalm 127:1a).

In other words, it is a waste of time to try to build anything apart from God. Jesus said that a wise man would build his house upon the rock. When the storm comes, the house will stand because its foundation is God. Why would God ask us to build our houses upon Him? God asks us to build upon Him because He wants to set us up for a victory in everything we do. Unless He has something to work with, our plans will never succeed and our houses will collapse.

It is a demonstration of God's love to us that He willingly sows Himself into our lives so that we can succeed. In John 3:16, one of the most quoted verses in the New Testament, God declares the extent of His love for this world. The reason this verse is so well known by believers is because it contains God's perfect plan for saving mankind.

For God so loved the world that He gave His only begotten Son, that whoever believes in Him should not perish but have everlasting life (John 3:16).

God did not simply forgive man, nor did He tell man how he could succeed on his own. He was not being difficult; He just knew it would not work. God knew that the only way He could draw near to man was if there was something in man to draw God there. In order for God to forgive mankind their many trespasses, God had to sow a God-seed into mankind. That seed was Jesus, whose name in Hebrew is *Yeshua*. When God sowed Himself, He had a very specific harvest in mind. He knew that if He sowed His only begotten Son, that seed would have to produce after its own kind. Therefore God was sowing for millions of children.

God's pattern of sowing should be the example that we live by as His children. In order to reap a God-harvest, we have to sow a God-seed with a God-assignment.

When we sow a God-seed with a God-assignment we will gain a God-harvest.

GOD SAVES GOD

And He saw that there was no man, and was astonished that there was no one to intercede; then His own arm brought salvation to Him, and His righteousness upheld Him (Isaiah 59:16 NASB).

Do you see what this verse is saying. God's own arm brought salvation to God and God's righteousness upheld God. Notice first how God was looking for a man who was righteous, who would intercede for Israel, God's people. God obviously had expectation that He would find someone, because the Word says He was astonished when He found no one! Therefore, because He could not work with Himself within a person to bring salvation, He worked with Himself to bring Himself salvation. God stretched out His righteous right arm and upheld Himself. God saved Himself! Even though we know that God doesn't need to be saved, this verse shows us that God is looking for Himself within His sons and daughters, and where He finds Himself He rescues and saves Himself. God is interested in protecting what is of His nature and character.

∽∽∽∽

God's right arm brought salvation for Himself.

∽∽∽∽

GOD IN HEAVEN WORKING WITH GOD ON EARTH

Jesus knew who He was. Jesus knew exactly what was in Him. He never had an inferiority complex or an insecurity issue. He knew His identity. He said, "*When you've seen Me, you've seen the Father. I and My Father are one*" (see John 14:9; 10:30). God in Heaven was bound to God on earth because of the principles of attraction, reciprocity, and seedtime and harvest that operate within the intimacy of God working with God (see Eph. 1:10). God sowed the seed of His Son all the while expecting that seed to reproduce over and over and over again. The Scripture makes it very clear that we are born again of the seed of Christ (the Messiah).

> *But to as many as did receive and welcome Him, He gave the authority (power, privilege, right) to become the children of God, that is, to those who believe in (adhere to, trust in, and rely on) His name—who owe their birth neither to bloods, nor to the will of the flesh [that of physical impulse] nor to the will of man [that of a natural father], but to God. [They are born of God!]* (John 1:12-13 AMP).

Born of God

When a baby is born, we have somewhat of an expectation as to what that child will be like, do we not? We say things like, "She's got her mother's eyes," or "That one looks just like his dad." We can immediately see the physical attributes, which were passed on to the child from its parents. As the child grows, the soulical characteristics of the parents will begin to show in the child also. If the mother is loud and quick-tempered, the child will begin to manifest these same traits. In the previous passage, John is drawing a comparison between the natural birth of children and the spiritual birth of the sons and daughters of God. John makes it clear that we are not born because of fleshly impulse or the will of a natural father; rather we are born of the seed of God. The Word of God has been planted in us and has become flesh, transforming us into new creatures. We are born of God and as we grow in Him from glory to glory, we bear His image more clearly.

Peter also explains this process through the inspiration of the Holy Spirit:

Having been born again, not of corruptible seed but of incorruptible, through the word of God which lives and abides forever (1 Peter 1:23).

God's Word endures forever. Do we really believe that? Do we believe that every one of the words that God has spoken still exists, is still moving forward, like a sound wave through time? Do we comprehend that God spoke our salvation into existence? Unless God had spoken it, salvation would have never come to us! Yet He has said, "I will deliver them; I will make them My people. I will set up a King to rule in righteousness over My people, and none will make them afraid anymore." We have been born of incorruptible seed, the seed of God, and Christ was the firstborn among many brethren.

Discovering our true identity in the
image of God attracts God!

God's Word will work in our lives only to the degree that we value, respect, and honor His Word. If we take God's Word lightly, not applying to our lives the things we know to be true, we should never expect the power of those words to have any effect on us. *Unless the vision of God's Word possesses you, you will never possess its fulfillment.* Jesus explains this principle to His disciples in Mark:

> *Then He said to them, "Take heed what you hear. With the same measure you use, it will be measured to you; and to you who hear, more will be given. For whoever has, to him more will be given; but whoever does not have, even what he has will be taken away from him"* (Mark 4:24-25).

When we accept God's Word, the power of that Word will flourish in our lives, filling us with the abundance that comes from seeing God come to pass in our lives. This Law, that the more we give in to God's Word, the more of it we will have, can release a volcano in your life. Understanding this principle will cause you to see the Word in a whole different light. The basic principle that I want to convey to you is that God has chosen to bind Himself to His Word, so that He will not do anything contrary to His Word; He is bound by His own integrity to bring it to pass. This means we can take God at His Word!

We do not have to wonder if we are praying God's will if we pray God's Word. I see this cyclical nature of God all the way from

Genesis to Revelation. Once again, in the following verse note how the Word is Yeshua, the Christ.

He was clothed with a robe dipped in blood, and His name is called The Word of God (Revelation 19:13).

Jesus is the Word that came in the flesh. He manifested God's glory, doing great signs and wonders, healing all those who were oppressed of the devil. He demonstrated God's character and nature in the flesh. It was through Him that God created all things.

And to make all see what is the fellowship of the mystery, which from the beginning of the ages has been hidden in God who created all things through Jesus Christ; to the intent that now the manifold wisdom of God might be made known by the church to the principalities and powers in the heavenly places, according to the eternal purpose which He accomplished in Christ Jesus our Lord (Ephesians 3:9-11).

Jesus is the Lamb slain before the foundation of the world. God spoke the salvation of mankind before He ever created the earth. Before God started start, He had already released the power that would restore all creation to its original perfection. Everything is held together by the Word of God; if God had never spoken it, it would not exist. All things are a direct product of the Word of God.

He is the sole expression of the glory of God [the Light-being, the out-raying or radiance of the divine], and He is the perfect image of [God's] nature, upholding and maintaining and guiding and propelling the universe by His mighty word of power. When He had by offering Himself accomplished our cleansing of sins and riddance of guilt, He sat down at the right hand of the divine Majesty on high (Hebrews 1:3 AMP).

Jesus, who is the express image of the Father, is now moving all things forward by His Word. Just as Hebrews 11:3 says that by faith we understand that the worlds were and are being created by a Word from God, we can believe that when we speak the Word of God our worlds are being formed around it. Why? Because God is bound to perform His Word, therefore we can always expect that everything around us will be transformed by our obedience to the Word of God. The only thing that is final is God's Word. If our circumstances do not look like the Word of God, we should be getting ready for a change in circumstances! God has the last word in everything.

> *In the beginning [before all time] was the Word (Christ), and the Word was with God, and the Word was God Himself. He was present originally with God. All things were made and came into existence through Him; and without Him was not even one thing made that has come into being. ... He came into the world, and though the world was made through Him, the world did not recognize Him [did not know Him]* (John 1:1-3,10 AMP).

This Scripture paints a picture for us of the intimacy that God has with Himself. God is a family; for this reason God created the man and the woman to manifest the kind of love relationship that God has within Himself. Just as the man and the woman are united in the act of common conception, so God is united within Himself to produce children after Him. Just as the woman carries the seed of her child within her womb, so God carries the seed of His Word within Himself. He cares for the Word, watches over it, seeing that it grows to full completion, and then births it into existence. What you see is an active relationship of a spiritual kind of intimacy. The Word was with God. The Word was also in communion with God; and God produced His entire creation through that Word. The International Standard Bible Encyclopedia states, "The Word was in eternity…not merely God's coeternal fellow, but the eternal God's self."[2]

Now let's paint a picture of the intimacy that exists between the Father, the Son, and the Holy Spirit. They are one. Their bond to each other is demonstrated in the Hebrew word echad. This word carries the sense of absolute unity. Taking two liquids and pouring them into each other, to the point that both liquids adhere to a new form, best demonstrate this word. They are no longer the liquid they were when they began; they have combined to become something completely new. This is the relationship that God has with Himself. Amazingly, God is calling us into the exact same unity and intimacy with Him that He has within Himself. As His children, we are called to walk out the reality of the most intimate place—where we are in complete union with Him.

CONCLUSION

In this chapter we have covered some very important truths. Let's go over the key ideas again, so we can get them firmly planted in our hearts.

- God and His Word are one; in fact, the Word is God. Scripture promises us that every Word, which God has spoken, will not return to Him void; rather, they will accomplish the purpose for which God sent them.

- God's Word is a seed that has the potential to produce God's very nature and character in our lives. When we believe and receive the Word of God, we can expect that our lives will take on the manifestation of that Word.

- When we believe that by Jesus' stripes we were healed, our bodies will manifest healing.

- The principle of seedtime and harvest is the process that God has chosen to spread His Kingdom all over the earth. Through this natural law, we see that God sowed Himself into the earth when He sent His only begotten Son to die for our sins. Because He sowed His Son, God has reaped the manifestation of His Son in millions of humans all over the earth for hundreds of years.

- Just as God and His Word are one, we also can experience the power of true unity with God by believing and receiving His Word, and by allowing that Word transform us into the image of God's Son.

TIMELESS TRUTHS FROM CHAPTER TWO

- A God who does not speak is no God at all.

- When God speaks He puts something of Himself in every word.

- To whom much is given, much is required.

- God only blesses what He sees of Himself in us.

- We need a God-seed or a God-word to be planted in our hearts. Only a God-seed or a God-word will produce a God-result.

- When we sow a God-seed with a God-assignment we will gain a God-harvest.

- God's right arm brought salvation for Himself.

ENDNOTES

1. David H. Stern, *Jewish New Testament Commentary* (Clarksville, MD: Jewish New Testament Publications, 1992).

2. James Orr, ed., "Person of Christ, 4-5," *International Standard Bible Encyclopedia*, accessed on the Internet at: http://www.searchgodsword.org/enc/isb/view.cgi?number=T6826.

CHAPTER THREE

The Spirit and the Word

A PICTURE OF GOD AT WORK

MOST Christians are aware that the New Covenant was originally penned in the Greek language. Nevertheless, what too many are oblivious to is the fact that Greek was merely the language the authors chose for the sake of wider readability throughout the Roman Empire. At the time of the birth of the church, all educated people spoke Greek, and because of the spread of Greek culture through Alexander the Great, almost all uneducated people spoke something called *koine* Greek, a simpler and cruder form of that language. For the sake of reaching as many people as possible, Paul and the other New Testament writers used Greek as their language of choice.

Yet, while the actual words were Greek, all of the background and thought behind the words chosen were of Hebrew origin. One reason for this is because the only Bible that Jesus and the apostles knew, studied, and taught from was written in Hebrew. As a result, it is important to look at the New Covenant through Hebrew eyes, since it was written by Jews with a Hebrew mind-set.

One of the differences between the Hebrew and the Greek relates to the importance of the verb in the sentence. Hebrew thought is very action oriented. Even in the way Hebrew sentences are constructed, the verb is often placed first. The action is at a place of emphasis. This focus on the action can even be conveyed conceptually in a kind of picture-image form. Hebrew words are best described through pictures because their meaning tends to run much deeper than a simple definition. For example, take a closer look at the word "made" in the following verses:

*In the beginning was the Word, and the Word was with God, and the Word was God. He was in the beginning with God. All things were **made** through Him, and without Him nothing was **made** that was **made** (John 1:1-3).*

Remember, behind these verses is a Jewish man who grew up reading and speaking Hebrew. He is a Hebrew of Hebrews. He does not think like a Gentile because he has never been one. John was a Jewish fisherman turned disciple of Jesus, not a Greek philosopher or scholar. We need to find out what John meant to portray in a Jewish context. The Hebrew word that stands behind the Greek word for "made" is *ginomai*; it means, "to cause to be, to come into being, to become." Combining our knowledge of Hebrew and Greek, we read that word "made" and can immediately see a picture of God working with His hands to cause something to have form and substance. We know from the above verses that God worked with His Word to give the whole universe form and substance, which is God working with God.

Remember, God's Word is not like the word of human beings. God has perfect integrity and a purpose for every word He speaks. All non-regenerated people with whom we deal in day-to-day life have a fallen nature. They perpetuate their nature with their words. Because they have never experienced real life, as in the life-giving power of the Holy Spirit, they only know death, and therefore, they are continually speaking death with their mouths. They speak negatively over their children, calling them stupid, and telling them they will never amount to anything. They expect bad things to happen to them, like cancer and diabetes, and live with an underlying fear of the circumstances that they speak with their mouths. They have never been taught that life and death are in the power of the tongue, and those who love it, eat the fruit of it (see Prov. 18:21).

As I mentioned in the previous chapter, satan uses the principles of planting and harvesting by planting thoughts of deception in people's minds. Their words are the seeds that, when they are full grown, give birth to sin, and sin to death. God, on the other hand, takes His words very seriously.

It would be helpful to get the following principle ingrained in your spirit:

∿◉∾

The Word is God's resumé; it is
His vision, purpose, and will.

∿◉∾

As we discussed in Chapter Two, we know that the Word is God. God and His Word are one. In light of this knowledge, John 1:1 could be read, "In the beginning was God, and God was with God, and God was God." Looking at it like this may seem redundant; however, it paints a vital picture of the God-working-with-God relationship that exists right now in the heavenlies. God is at work with

Himself. It is a picture that I believe God wants burned in our memories forever.

I have heard it said that a picture paints a thousand words. Yet I see the opposite demonstrated by God's Word. Every word He speaks creates new visions, new imaginations. God's Word is so alive and full of Himself that it literally paints a thousand pictures.

A Word from God is worth a thousand pictures.

In His essence, God is not limited in any way. He is all-powerful, His mercy endures forever, and His knowledge is endless. Picture yourself entering a magnificent doorway adorned with the finest carved facade that opens into a stunning banquet hall with a long table covered with rare delicacies. Though the wonderful table and delicious food could hold your attention for eternity, you also notice that there are doors going in every direction from the banquet hall. You decide to investigate, and you find more halls ornately decorated, with beautiful paintings and statues, and more rooms full of treasures of every kind, more doors leading to more hallways, which end in more rooms, all more wondrous than the last, and still more doorways. This maze of intrigue and beauty does not begin to fully express God's knowledge and wisdom. They are like an endless series of opportunities and paths that seem to go on forever. God is so massive!

In fact, the more we get into God, the more we realize how little we really know. If we took all of the wisdom and knowledge gathered about God by His children since the beginning of time and added it all together and put it in a library and read all the books written, we would still only have not even a milliliter, not even a drop in the bucket, compared to the vastness of God's mighty mind!

The sad truth is that some of the things we have been taught all of our lives in the church building actually have nothing to do with the actual knowledge of God; some teachings could even be classified as the opposite of God's knowledge. The Body of Christ has got to come to grips with the reality that hundreds of years ago, the so-called "church" became more or less a political institution. On that day, the church handed over its God-given assignment to spread true revelatory knowledge and wisdom; in its place they received the cheap counterfeit of secularism and relativism.

When we approach God's Word with the desire to receive the revelatory knowledge promised to us as part of our inheritance, there will probably be doctrine from our religious past that will have to be unlearned, stripped away, and tossed out with the rest of the trash, in order to grasp the things of God. A prime example of false ideas that have permeated the church and been spread for hundreds of years is this: Many organized religions have tried to strip Christianity of its power and Jewish heritage. They have tried to make Jesus a Roman or a European. Jesus, whose Hebrew name was Yeshua, was of the tribe of Judah, of the line of King David. He was not Latin! He was a Jew.

Recently I have been aggressively pursuing Jewish studies, including Hebrew language and thought. I have had experiences in my studies at home, when tears would start running down my cheeks as God began to unveil the great revelations hidden in the original language that God chose to communicate His Word through. Though God can and does reveal Himself to us through the modern languages that we speak, there is something very special about the meaning of the original words.

BRINGING HIMSELF TO PASS

Let's go back to John 1:1 again. I know, we've been there before, but I want to make sure that everything that God has to say is said. Sometimes, He says to me, "Warren, go back and read that verse again. I'm not through with that one yet." It would be wrong for me to rush ahead to something else and miss the heartbeat of God right in front of me. So let's look closely at John 1:1, and see if there isn't another great revelation just waiting to be discovered within those simple words:

In the beginning was the Word... (John 1:1).

Often the first three words of this verse are sort of skipped over, as if the biblical author was simply looking for a place to start and thought "in the beginning" was as good a place as any! How foolish it is to look at God's Word as if the little details do not matter. Every word, its placing in the original text, and its biblical context, literal and historical, is very important—too important to look over.

I like the way Dr. Myles Munroe defines "beginning" in his book, *Releasing Your Potential*:

Everything that was, and is, was in God. In the beginning God created the heavens and the earth (Genesis 1:1). He pulled everything He made out of Himself. Indeed, the beginning was in God before it began. God started start. If the book of Genesis had started with Genesis 1:0, it might have read, "Before there was a beginning, there was God. Before there was a creation, there was a Creator. Before any-thing, there was God."[1]

In this quote, Dr. Munroe focuses in on just how much every-thing depends on God as the Creator of the universe. If "He pulled everything He made out of Himself," as Dr. Munroe says, God was truly displaying the power that is contained within His own imagination. God took His ideas and made them a reality. What would creation be without this demonstration of God's unique abilities? It wouldn't be much to speak of! Even before God began speaking, His Word was already alive; the Word was prepared to go forth and accomplish His will. His Word could not fail, because the Word is God.

The Bible makes it clear that we are totally hopeless without God. That is why the book that He wrote focuses on His mighty intervention in the lives of men and women. From the very beginning, when God made clothes of animal skin for Adam and Eve, to the story of Noah, where God saved the righteous man and his family from utter destruction; from God speaking to Moses from the burning bush, even though Moses was a convicted murderer, to God's great mercy for Samson, we can see God moving in and among His people, both to will and to do all that He had planned.

The revelation in the names of God should penetrate our hearts with God's preeminence: He is the Alpha and Omega, the First and the Last. The writer of Hebrews even describes Jesus as being the Author and Finisher of our faith. Out of His own vastness and beauty, He created all things to be a reflection of Him, and from His mighty greatness will come the completion of all things, until everything in Heaven and all things on earth are in perfect unity in Him.

God can bring to pass only what He finds
of Himself inside you.

I'm set in my spirit to repeat this truth to you until we all have it ingrained in our brains. The Bible is the only true success manual in existence for anything mankind will ever do. Some might say that the Scripture does not apply to the natural life; it is only for spiritual insight. After all we don't want to be so heavenly minded that we are no earthly good! Let me tell you something right now: That is a lie from the devil, and it stinks! The truth is that *if we are truly heavenly minded we will be of earthly good*. Paul says in Colossians 3:2-3:

> *Set your mind on things above, not on things on the earth. For you died, and your life is hidden with Christ in God.*

Focusing on the things of God will bring greater clarity in every natural circumstance that comes into your life! When you have His Word written on your hearts, you will also know what to say to every circumstance that comes your way. Did you know that God wants you to succeed? It's true! That is the reason He gave you His Word. Success is already built into the Word because the power is already there for His Word to come to pass. All we have to do is take that Word and apply it to our lives. If we miss the importance of His Word, if we do not take the power of it to heart, we will try to force God into blessing our own plans, instead of conforming our plans to His Word, which is His will. He is not interested in bringing our plans and desires to pass, unless they are plans and desires that come directly from Him.

Paul makes it clear in His letter to the Ephesians that God will bring His will to pass—not just part of it, *all* of His purposes are being worked out to His glory.

> *In Him we were also chosen, having been predestined according to the plan of Him who works out everything in conformity with the purpose of His will* (Ephesians 1:11 NIV).

Do not allow yourself to get sidetracked on the word *predestined*. Some denominations have created whole doctrines from this verse, claiming that God has chosen some to live and some to die, some to have success and some to have failure, some for Heaven and some for hell. However, this teaching totally nullifies the God of Covenant, destroying man's responsibility to keep his end of the mutual alliance he has with God through the blood of Jesus. In fact, quite the opposite is true.

When we choose to step into the power of God working with God, we are immediately predestined for success. Only God's Word has no choice but to never fail.

The power of God's Word—God working with God—is already at work, commanding all things to conform to His perfect will and purpose. In other words, *He is out to bring Himself to pass.* Remember what we stated earlier: *God's Word is His resumé; it is His vision, purpose, and will.* In other words, if you want to know what God is doing, what He wants to do, where He is going, and where He wants you to go, ask His Spirit to reveal it to you from His Word. It's all there! God works out everything in conformity to His will because His will and His Word are one.

What is the Bible saying? God is going to work with His Word because the Word is God.

> *Now this is the confidence that we have in Him, that if we ask anything according to His will, He hears us* (1 John 5:14).

God only hears God's will.

Up to this point in the chapter, we have been going over some of the most foundational God-working-with-God principles. This may seem redundant to you; I promise you, however, the key to learning is hearing a thing repeated over and over again, until it can be recited back to the teacher. Now I want to begin to apply these principles to the relationship that God has with man. If God only works with Himself, how does this affect the shape of our personal lives? It's simple! Do you remember the story of Joshua?

After the death of Moses the servant of the Lord, it came to pass that the Lord spoke to Joshua the son of Nun, Moses' assistant, saying: "Moses My servant is dead. Now therefore, arise, go over this Jordan, you and all this people, to the land which I am giving to them—the children of Israel. Every place that the sole of your foot will tread upon I have given you, as I said to Moses. From the wilderness and this Lebanon as far as the great river, the River Euphrates, all the land of the Hittites, and to the Great Sea toward the going down of the sun, shall be your territory. No man shall be able to stand before you all the days of your life; as I was with Moses, so I will be with you. I will not leave you nor forsake you. Be strong and of good courage, for to this people you shall divide as an inheritance the land which I swore to their fathers to give them. Only be strong and very courageous, that you may observe to do according to all the law which Moses My servant commanded you; do not turn from it to the right hand or to the left, that you may prosper wherever you go. This Book of the Law shall not depart from your mouth, but you shall meditate in it day and night, that you may observe to do according to all that is written in it. For then you will make your way prosperous, and then you will have good success. Have I not commanded you? Be strong and of good courage; do not be afraid, nor be dismayed, for the Lord your God is with you wherever you go" (Joshua 1:1-9).

Let's stop right here for a moment and look closely at these verses. What is it that God commands Joshua to do? He tells Joshua that *the key to his success is meditating on the words of God and not allowing them to depart from his mouth!* Interestingly enough, God does not promise that He will make Joshua's way prosperous if he keeps the Law; rather, the Lord promises that Joshua will make his own way prosperous if he speaks God's words instead of his own. It is so plain to see from this passage! The success of all we do is wrapped up in whether or not we live and breathe the Word of God!

God commands Joshua to be strong and full of courage, affirming to him that He will keep His word. Because of Joshua's experience with Moses in the wilderness for 40 years, he knew that the God he served was full of integrity and was a performer of His Word. Joshua knew that the consequences of speaking and observing the Law of God were peace and victory in every situation. When we are careful to meditate on the Word of God, when we continually speak what God speaks instead of how we feel about what we see, we can be confident that God will send forth His Word to accomplish His purpose. *The measure to which the Word of God gets inside our hearts is the same measure to which God will bring it to pass.*

Hundreds of years before Jesus was born in Bethlehem, the Greeks developed a system of false gods and goddesses to whom they worshiped and sacrificed, just as the Jews sacrificed to YHWH. This order of divine beings was called the Pantheon; these beings were not anything like the God of the Hebrews, however. They displayed all kinds of human frailties and shortcomings. This mythology did not evolve by accident. It was in fact a demonic attack on the character of the one true God.

Often these beings were depicted in petty squabbles with each other. They had human emotional weaknesses and were often competing for man's affection. The real God has no such flaws of character. He is the fully sufficient One. Even though He is a jealous God, a consuming fire, His jealousy is pure and comes out of a desire to see His Word come to pass in our lives. YHWH does not have any of the shortcomings or faults that humans are subject to because of the fall. God does not have an inferiority complex. God does not have an insecurity problem. He has never had an identity crisis! To Moses He revealed Himself as, "I AM who I AM." Jesus made this same claim, when He said to the Pharisees, *"Before Abraham was, I AM"* (John 8:58). This was a God-working-with-God connection between the Father and the Son; the communication that the Father had to the Son was God speaking to Himself. Jesus never spoke anything but what He heard the Father saying. When Jesus opened His mouth, God came out of it. God loves to communicate with Himself because He knows that His communication works. We will explain this further in a future book called, *GWWG: God Hears Himself.*

"I AM who I AM" leaves us with an astounding picture of a God who is self-sustaining and confident that His Word will always work. Knowing who God really is will bring everything else in our lives into perfect focus. The Word of God is like a magnifying glass that we hold up to our lives. The Word of God makes it easy for us to see all of the details clearly, helping us to understand who God says we really are, and how we fit into God's grand plan for His creation. Rather than trying to bring God down to our level of human failure (as the Greeks did), we can actually allow Him to pull us up to His level of greatness. When we choose to look at God through the clarity of His Word, rather than through the messed up circumstances of our past or through the frustration of our present or the confusion of our future, we will find that all of who He is, is much bigger than everything that we are. We can begin to grasp that His plan, purpose, and perfect will includes us! Only through the Word can we discover our origin in God.

> *Remember the former things of old, for I am God, and there is no other; I am God and there is none like Me, declaring the end from the beginning, and from ancient times things that are not yet done, saying, "My counsel shall stand, and I will do all My pleasure"* (Isaiah 46:9-10).

Have you ever thought about what God's pleasure is? What does God enjoy? Is it possible for us as humans to bring God pleasure? Of course it is! It brought God pleasure to create you; if it hadn't, He would have never done it! It brought God pleasure to put the stars in place and to create all the fish and animals. God's creation brings Him pleasure for one reason. He created the natural world to operate the same as a mirror.

Have you ever bent over the grass at the edge of a lake and looked down into the water? If the water is clear, you will see your own face wiggling and rippling up at you. Doesn't it just make you smile? Look, there you are, smiling already! When God looks at creation, guess what He sees? He glimpses the reflection of the most handsome, wisest, most joyful, most exquisite face in the whole universe: His own! This brings God much pleasure. The desire of every child of God should be to show God a reflection of Himself.

When we believe, speak, and act upon the Word of God, we are showing our Father in Heaven that we want to be just like Him; we want His kingdom to come and His will to be done, that all of His Word may come to pass in our lives. Is this the desire of your heart? If it is, then God is smiling at you right now because you are bringing Him pleasure.

Have you ever looked at a blueprint for a house? A blueprint shows the builder the exact pattern that the architect wants for the house he is creating. A blueprint is always made to scale; every room is just the right measurement, every wall is just the right height, every doorway is just the right width. If the blueprint is not drawn correctly, the house will be faulty. The foundation might not be perfectly square, or the water pump may be too far away from the house. In order for the outcome to be just right, the plan needs to be followed without fail. Is it not intriguing that God's Word works just like a blueprint? Like a builder, if we do not work God's Word His way then the end result will not be God's perfect will! What He speaks has to be what He means to happen, and for His will to happen, His Word must be followed without fail. His desires will come to absolute fruition, whether we believe it or not.

The question is, do we want to be part of God's will coming to pass? If we do, then we must believe that God's council will stand. We must step into God working with God. This is our responsibility, not God's, because He never changes.

Consider the Theory of Relativity, discovered and developed by Albert Einstein, which in simplicity is a scientific demonstration of the reality of God working with God. How so? Jesus taught that He was the light that was coming into the world, and Einstein concluded that light is always constant; it is the only unchangeable thing. Jesus said, and we proclaim, that He is the same, yesterday, today, and forever. The light that God sent into the world will never go out and will never change. Einstein proved God's constancy and presented it in a way that it could not be denied by the scientific world. The Light of the World never changes.

FRAMED BY THE WORD

Hebrews chapter 11 is sometimes called the faith hall of fame because it is full of the stories of men and women who walked out a mighty faith in God that caused them to triumph over the most dire circumstances. From Enoch, Abraham, and Sarah, to Moses, Deborah, and David, the biblical author recounts to us the overcoming children of God, who left behind what was comfortable to them in order to pursue the will of God. Though their faith was amazing, I would like to change the nickname of this chapter to the God-working-with-God hall of fame, if you don't mind. God spoke His Word to His child, who then believed it as true and ran with it. God moved on behalf of Himself to bring that Word to pass, and so those who believed were victorious over their enemies and over their own fears. These amazing men and women believed that what God said He would do. Faith, or our ability to believe in what has no material evidence, enables us to see all things coming into being through God's Word.

By faith we understand that the worlds were framed by the word of God, so that the things which are seen were not made of things which are visible (Hebrews 11:3).

This verse reveals that by having faith, you can clearly understand the role of God's Word in creation. Be careful not to confuse the role of faith in this verse. God did not create all things through faith, as some teach. God does not need faith because He has perfect vision. He can see all things, their birth and their completion. God knows the finish of every Word He has ever spoken. Faith is only needed in the absence of declaring power. God did not have faith that light would come into existence; rather, He declared it to be so and it was. Faith enables us as His children to begin to see things the way He sees them, instead of limiting ourselves to the blurry vision that guilt causes us to have. When guilt is dealt with through the blood, we can start looking at things through our Father's eyes. Clearly, this verse teaches us that all the worlds were framed by the words of God.

The Greek word for "framed" is *katartizo* (kat-ar-tid'zo), which means "to complete thoroughly, i.e. repair (literally or figuratively) or adjust; fit, frame, mend, (make) perfect (-ly join together), prepare, restore." Once again, let's look at the Hebrew concept behind this Greek word, for a better understanding of what the original audience would have grasped from the text.

The Hebrew word that stands behind the Greek is *yatsar*. This word provides us with a picture of the master potter taking the clay and throwing it onto the wheel. In His mind, He can see the finished product already. So what does He do? He cuts away everything that does not conform to the image, and with His hands, He molds the clay into the plan and design that He purposed for it.

The Greek word for "worlds" used in the Book of Hebrews is *aion*; the primary stress of this word is time in its unbroken duration. Think of the implications of this word! In the Book of Hebrews, the biblical author is describing how God molded the worlds with His Word into the exact purpose that He declared for it; except, He is not talking about worlds, as in Earth, Venus, and Mars. The author of Hebrews is speaking of cultural periods of time. The amazing thing is that God desires us to frame, radically alter, our worlds with His Word!

Throughout Scripture, God always used a man to speak His Word: When He wanted the sun to stand still, God used the voice of Joshua. When He wanted to convict King David of adultery and murder, He spoke through Nathan the prophet. When He wanted to give His law to the Israelites, God spoke through His servant Moses. God always spoke words through people to convey His truth. God desires to declare life through your voice to radically reshape and alter the places and circumstances in which you live, by speaking His Word over your worlds. Like a potter, He can take our lives and conform them to His purpose and His will.

FACE TO FACE

Once again, let's return to John 1:1. There is something more, an amazing revelation that God has unveiled to me within those words, and now I want to show it to you! The Montgomery Translation of John 1:1 reads, *"In the beginning was the Word and **the Word was face to face with God** and the Word was God."* I told you! There is something more to see here. This translation is full of insight, because it draws a picture in the mind of two mighty Spirits, standing very close together, looking at each other in the eye. They share something very important in common with each other; for they are both God, divine Spirits, fully sufficient and full of glory.

Many translations of the Bible use the word "with" to translate the Greek preposition *pros*, which can also be translated as "toward, into, to, unto, or turned into." This word always implies mutual fellowship and intercommunication. Thus we see that in the beginning, God and His Word were sharing close, intimate communication with each other. The Father and the Son were knit together in love.

When we look at the second verse of Genesis, we see this same closeness and intimacy that John describes in his Gospel. In this instance, we encounter the third person of the Trinity in relationship with creation.

The earth was without form, and void; and darkness was on the face of the deep. And the Spirit of God was hovering over the face of the waters (Genesis 1:2).

This verse demonstrates to us the importance of knowing the original language. Only by studying the meaning of the Hebrew words will we begin to see a connection between the close intercommunication between the Father and His Word shown to us in John 1:1, and the Spirit of God who moved upon the face of the waters. God wants us to see how His Spirit and His Word intricately worked together to create all things. It was their face-to-face relationship that brought about the conception of the earth. Note what Hebrew scholar Dr. Douglas Wheeler has to comment on the above verse: "The key word here is 'face of.' If we look at this statement in the original Hebrew, we would see that the phrase translated 'upon the face of' is in Hebrew 'al-peney.' This particular expression can mean, 'to turn oneself, to turn towards and to face, to be in the front of or forepart. It also means to be face to face and in the presence of.'"[2]

In this Scripture we can see that the Spirit of God was moving face to face with the water, awaiting the seed of God to be planted within it so that creation could come into being. The Hebrew word *al-peney* depicts an intimate communication, a face-to-face encounter, between God's Spirit and what is about to be created. In order for creation to come into being, the Spirit of God had to work with the seed of God's Word to produce God's will. An act of intimacy was about to occur. God was about to produce something from and of Himself.

We have thoroughly shown you how God works in an intimate way with His Word. This truth is demonstrated all through Scripture, as God promises that His Word will stand forever, and that He has exalted it above His name. The Bible teaches us that the Word is Jesus, God the Son. Jesus never claimed to be separate from God. He never took credit for any of the awesome miracles that He did. His only claim, to which He had a right, was that He was one with, and continually in intimate communication with, His Father. Jesus could not have been separate from God in any way. He was and is God. The movements and actions of the Father are the movements and actions of the Son. They are face to face and are progressing simultaneously.

Now I want to introduce to you the role of God the Holy Spirit in relationship to God bringing all of His Word to pass. You see, without the movement of the Holy Spirit upon the water, creation would not and could not have ever happened. The Holy Spirit always works in close union and agreement with the Word.

Thousands of years ago, the earth was barren and covered with darkness. Nothing that we know now of the earth existed then. There was silence all around. Yet the earth was not without life, for God was moving upon the face of that deep darkness. His purposes for earth, which was void and empty, made the air thick and rich. The Spirit of the Most High was awaiting the Word of God. As He hovered over the face of the deep, the Holy Spirit brooded over the promise of God's will, as if God was focusing His divine concentration on the release of power that was about to occur. As the Spirit moved upon the water, God was creating a working relationship between Himself and what was about to become His creation. Then, out of the deep of the darkness came the voice of the Creator, as He proclaimed, "Let there be LIGHT!"

As He spoke, His Word and His Spirit immediately came into unity with each other; out of that place of perfect intimacy, creation was birthed, a perfect reflection, a mighty replica, a master copy of all that God is and all that He has. When I studied the Hebrew word for "spirit," I discovered something very interesting. The word for spirit in Hebrew is *ruwach*. When it is used in the noun form, it can mean the Spirit of God or heavenly spirits, such as angels; it can also mean wind, tempest, the life or breath of a person, and the soul. When it is used as a verb, however, it connotes touch, smell, and a quickening of all of the senses, plus an enjoyment of the experience.

It is amazing to me how God's Spirit is described as manifesting in extremely physical ways. The union of God to Himself, the Spirit of God working with the Word of God, brought about the conception of all things created, a physical world, full of smells, tastes, sounds, and textures for man to experience as a demonstration of God's nature and character. In Genesis 1:2, He is called the *Ruwach Elohim*, the Spirit of the Creator; and in Psalm 51:12 and Isaiah 63:10-11, He is called the *Ruwach Hakedesh*, the Holy Spirit:

> *But they rebelled and grieved His Holy Spirit; so He turned Himself against them as an enemy, and He fought against them. Then he remembered the days of old, Moses and his people, saying: "Where is He who brought them up out of the sea with the shepherd of His flock? Where is He who put His Holy Spirit within them"* (Isaiah 63:10-11).

How did the children of Israel grieve the Holy Spirit? If you study this chapter, along with many other passages spoken by the prophets, Isaiah makes it clear that their disobedience was in their rejection of the Word of God spoken to them through the Law of Moses and through the mouths of the prophets. They refused to believe and receive the Word so that they might enter into the bond that God has with Himself.

By whatever revelation name we choose to call Him, the Spirit of the Most High God is still working with the Word of God to transform us into the image of the Father. When we choose to believe and receive the Word of God as a seed of His divine nature in our lives, we have the opportunity to experience the spiritual birth that always takes place when the Word of God and the Spirit of God come into perfect unity and intimacy.

The most awesome expression of this truth happened when a young woman from the town of Nazareth chose to believe and receive the Word of God as true. When the angel announced to Mary what was going to take place within her womb, Mary chose to accept God's Word, thus allowing the God-seed to be planted in her.

Then Mary said, "Behold the maidservant of the Lord! Let it be to me according to your word." And the angel departed from her (Luke 1:38).

What did it take for that seed, the Word, to become flesh in Mary's womb, so that God the Son could be birthed into the earth to accomplish God's will and purpose for mankind? It took Mary's willingness, first and foremost. Secondly, it took the Holy Spirit's coming into unity with the Word, so that conception could take place. Do you remember what the angel prophesied?

*Then the angel said to her, "Do not be afraid, Mary, for you have found favor with God. And behold, you will conceive in your womb and bring forth a Son, and shall call His name JESUS. He will be great, and will be called the Son of the Highest; and the Lord God will give Him the throne of His father David. And He will reign over the house of Jacob forever, and of His kingdom there will be no end." Then Mary said to the angel, "How can this be, since I do not know a man?" And the angel answered and said to her, "**The Holy Spirit will come upon you**, and the power of the Highest will overshadow you; therefore, also, that Holy One who is to be born will be called the Son of God"* (Luke 1:30-35).

Just as the Holy Spirit hovered over the face of the deep during the first creation in Genesis 1, God the Spirit came and hovered over Mary and began to work with the Word of God that she had received from the angel. He moved over her with tender mercy, love, and genuine intimacy, as God the Word became one with God the Spirit, and perfect conception took place. The Spirit of God waited until the God-seed had been planted within her, so that He could propel that Word into existence. Like two fluids being poured together, God became one with Himself within the woman, and out of that union, God began again with another perfect Adam: God took on flesh and became a man! This new creation was God's victory over the fall of man to sin and death, making a way through redemption for the conversion of the Gentiles to come to pass.

In Acts 10:44 we see that:

While Peter was still speaking these words, the Holy Spirit fell upon all those who heard the word.

While Peter preached the Word of God, that Word was received and believed by those who heard the Word. Immediately, the Spirit of God went to work with the Word of God, and a new creature was born. These new creatures spoke a new creature language. Just as it happened at the dawn of time, when God spoke the Word and the Spirit of God worked with that Word to create all things, the Holy Spirit fell upon all those who heard the anointed Word that Peter was speaking, and a new creature was born. In essence, He was saying, "I accomplished it once; I can accomplish it again! In the beginning, I spoke My Word out of nothing, and that Word came to pass. Within the council of My own will I created a man. He was both physical and divine. He was My exact image, the manifestation of My power and glory. It was his choice to rebel against My Word and fall from his place of perfection. Now, I have created Myself again! I spoke My Word; My Spirit hovered over it and gave it life; My Word became a flesh-and-bone body. For this reason, the Holy One within her was called the Son of God, for His obedience to My Word was the weapon that I used to destroy the rebellion that separated Me from all of My Sons!"

Jesus was the firstborn among many brethren; He is the Head and the Elder Brother of all God's children; He entered behind the veil one time for all, so that through His suffering many could be made perfect. As the High Priest after the order of Melchizedek, "*He Himself* [has become] *our peace, who has made both one, and has broken down the middle wall of separation*" (Eph. 2:14), the wall of disobedience and rejection of His Word, that has since the fall alienated us from the Father.

God works with us exactly the same way now as He did with Mary and Jesus. We hear the Word, receive the Word, the Spirit of God hovers over the Word, God works with Himself in us, and the harvest is birthed.

> *Therefore, just as through one man sin entered the world, and death through sin, and thus death spread to all men, because all sinned—(For until the law sin was in the world, but sin is not imputed when there is no law. Nevertheless death reigned from Adam to Moses, even over those who had not sinned according to the likeness of the transgression of Adam, who is a type of Him who was to come. But the free gift is not like the offense. For if by the one man's offense many died, much more the grace of God and the gift by the grace of the one Man, Jesus Christ, abounded to many. And the gift is not like that which came through the one who sinned. For the judgment which came from one offense resulted in condemnation, but the free gift which came from many offenses resulted in justification. For if by the one man's offense death reigned through the one, much more those who receive abundance of grace and of the gift of righteousness will reign in life through the One, Jesus Christ.) Therefore, as through one man's offense judgment came to all men, resulting in condemnation, even so through one Man's righteous act the free gift came to all men, resulting in justification of life* (Romans 5:12-18).

This is the mighty power of God working with God. Through it we can identify that our origin is not in the things of the flesh, of this world, or the corruption of sin and death! No, our origin is in God; and within the spoken Word of God lies the God-destiny that He has prepared for us since He first created man thousands of years ago! When we realize that the source of our being lies not in the natural resources of this world, but in God, we will begin to expect the supernatural power of God that split the Red Sea and turned the water into wine to manifest in and through us.

THE NATURE OF MIRACLES

Once the God-working-with-God principles are set in motion in your life, it will become obvious to you the awesome potential that God has placed within you by inundating your life with His Word. The church must grasp the preeminence of God's Word so that God's power can be released through us to minister to the nations. Both our origin and the release of God's miraculous power in our lives are tied to the intimate relationship between the Spirit of God and the Word. When Genesis says that the Spirit of God hovered over the waters, the biblical author is drawing a picture of a love relationship, as a mother has with a child.

In his *Hebrew-Chaldee Lexicon to the Old Testament*, H.W.F. Gesenius gives the following definition for hovering: "To be moved, affected, with the feeling of tender love, to cherish, to brood over as an eagle does her young ones, figuratively used of the Spirit of God, who brooded over the shapeless mass of the earth, cherishing and vivifying."[3]

In a place of perfect intimacy between God and Himself, the power of God is continually manifesting to conceive life. The powerful imagery of the eagle nestling down with her young one reveals to us the mother-like characteristics of God; this manifestation of those godly attributes best demonstrated by women is also evidence that God has everything within Himself to conceive within Himself the fulfillment of every Word He has ever spoken.

The New John Gill Exposition of the Entire Bible states clearly, "This same Spirit 'moved' or brooded upon the face of the waters, to impregnate them, as an hen upon eggs to hatch them, so he to separate the parts which were mixed together, and give them a quickening virtue to produce living creatures in them."[4]

It is interesting that God chose to manifest this process of intimacy within the creation of man: male and female. Now, these next paragraphs might make some people uncomfortable, but let's get real. Every natural process within our bodies was created to manifest God's glory, and the intimacy between a man and a woman within the confines of covenant does just this in an extremely pragmatic way. If we are not willing to discuss the areas of God's nature that make us uncomfortable, we will never experience those parts of His character in our lives.

Have you ever seen a picture of an unfertilized egg within a woman's ovary? Within that egg there exists half of the ingredients needed to make a baby. Half of its identity traits, half of its physical features, and half of its mental tendencies lie within the egg. It is impossible, however, for that egg to become anything more than what it is without a seed from the man. This seed was built to produce. Once it has been released, the seed is on a quest to become one with an egg, and it won't stop until its job is complete! It is as if the seed says, "I know my destiny. I can't be a baby without an egg; please get out of my way, so I can find one!" Only by physical manipulation, or the hand of God, can this process be stopped. Is it not intriguing that the egg cannot go out and find itself a seed? For the egg to become complete, it must rest where it can grow until the proper time for release.

Just look at the similarities between God working with God and the amazing process of human procreation! God sends forth the seed of His Word; it is on a quest to produce all that it was sent to do. The Word knows its destiny, yet without a willing heart to accept it and yield to it, the seed remains dormant and untapped. Once one person says, "Be it unto me according to Your Word," that seed will burrow deep into the inner man of that individual; it will begin to take on flesh, manifesting the fulfillment of God's Word in accordance with the individual's ability to yield to it. Of course it does take time for the Word to come to fruition in our lives, just as it takes time for a baby to fully develop within the womb of a woman.

Let's get to the point. There is but one natural way for a baby to be produced, one way for the seed to be released within the woman, in order for the egg and the seed to become one and take on new life. The only God-designed cause for pregnancy is the celebration of blood covenant between a man and his wife. God arranged that babies would be the product of an act of intimacy.

In like manner, there is but one way that God's Word, and consequently His power, will be birthed in our lives, and that is through intimacy with God. It is the same way that the Gentiles manifested the Word. They heard and received the Word, the Holy Spirit hovered over the Word that they received, and a new creature was born who spoke a new creature language.

Intimacy is the birthplace of miracles!

As the Word of God becomes deeply rooted in your heart, God's Spirit will come to brood over that Word as we saw in Acts 10:44-45. The miraculous power of God that is a direct consequence to His Word being birthed in your life is a manifestation of the care and love of the Holy Spirit for that Word. Do you remember the story in

Acts, when the people brought out their sick, just in case the shadow of Peter would pass over them?

So that they [even] kept carrying out the sick into the streets and placing them on couches and sleeping pads, [in the hope] that as Peter passed by, at least his shadow might fall on some of them (Acts 5:15 AMP).

Peter was so full of God that as he walked down the streets God's covenant children were attracted to the nature of God pouring out of him. The anointing that was flowing through his heart was rooted and grounded in love, and was producing great compassion which activated an overflow of the power of the Holy Spirit. The Word of God's good news must have spread throughout the whole region drawing God's covenant people to the area where God's apostles were manifesting the Kingdom of God.

In this we can see how God is attracted to God. As Peter passes by people , the Holy Spirit broods over the sick and lame as He did over the void and formless earth in Genesis chapter one. And just as God's life was poured out into the earth through the Word, God raises up the sick and lame because of the Word of God within Peter. Once again, God was intimately face to face with Himself and with His creation, as He worked mighty signs and wonders among the people. Emmanuel, God with us, was manifesting through His son Peter just as He had manifested through His Son Jesus. The key was a working relationship between God in Heaven and God in man.

It is probably obvious to you that the God we serve has always revealed Himself through miracles, signs, and wonders. He has always taken every opportunity to show Himself mighty and to do powerful works on behalf of His children. I believe that every time God performed a miracle in Scripture, whether it was through Elijah, when he raised the widow's son from the dead, or through Paul and the other apostles, God worked with the seed of His own nature and character within them to produce God-results. For the sake of understanding the nature of God's miraculous power, let's look more closely at the story of Elijah and the widow at Zarephath:

Then the word of the Lord came to him, saying, "Arise, go to Zarephath, which belongs to Sidon, and dwell there. See, I have commanded a widow there to provide for you." So he arose and went to Zarephath. And when he came to the gate of the city, indeed a widow was there gathering sticks. And he called to her and said, "Please bring me a little water in a cup, that I may drink." And as she was going to get it, he called to her and said, "Please bring me a morsel of bread in your hand." So she said, "As the Lord your God lives, I do not have bread, only a handful of flour in a bin, and a little oil in a jar; and see, I am gathering a couple of sticks that I may go in and prepare it for myself and my son, that we may eat it, and die." And Elijah said to her, "Do not fear; go and do as you have said, but make me a small cake from it first, and bring it to me; and afterward make some for yourself and your son. For thus says the Lord God of Israel: 'The bin of flour shall not be used up, nor shall the jar of oil run dry, until the day the Lord sends rain on the earth.'" So she went away and did according to the word of Elijah; and she and he and her household ate for many days. The bin of flour was not used up, nor did the jar of oil run dry, according to the word of the Lord which He spoke by Elijah. Now it happened after these things that the son of the woman who owned the house became sick. And his sickness was so serious that there was no breath left in him. So she said to Elijah, "What have I to do with you, O man of God? Have you come to me to bring my sin to remembrance, and to kill my son?" And he said to her, "Give me your son." So he took him out of her arms and carried him to the upper room where he was staying, and laid him on his own bed. Then he cried out to the Lord and said, "O Lord my God, have You also brought tragedy on the widow with whom I lodge, by killing her son?" And he stretched him-self out on the child three times, and cried out to the Lord and said, "O Lord my God, I pray, let this child's soul come back to him." Then the Lord heard the voice of Elijah; and the soul of the child came back to him, and he revived (1 Kings 17:8-22).

The widow woman of Zarephath was completely destitute and had resigned herself to death because of her poverty. She couldn't see past her circumstances, even to the next meal! Yet she knew in her heart that God had commanded her to serve the man of God and give all she had to him. God knew that she was in desperate need of His mighty power in her life. She received God's Word to answer God's man. He, God, was setting her up for miracle by thrusting her into a situation where she had to give everything she had away and trust that God would still provide for her family.

When Elijah showed up on the scene, he already knew her situation. But by looking through the eyes of God, he could see that her circumstances were about to change. Elijah said to the woman, "Feed me first." This story is overflowing with the principles of God working with God. God in man doing things that man cannot do but only God can do, placed a demand on a seed already under God's command. God worked with God, and the result was an overflow to the point that not only was that widow and her son saved but *nations* were saved.

In the same way, the more we receive the Word and the Spirit works with the Word, the more we will see overflow in the nature of miracles. (This will be expounded upon in a later volume of *God Working With God*.) The widow willingly gave to the man of God. We know that giving is part of God's nature because John 3:16 says, *"For God so loved the world, that He gave...."* The widow was obedient to the voice of God and walked out the nature of God, which resulted in an overflow of blessing in her life.

YOUR ANSWER IS IN THE WORD

God's Word has the potential of becoming flesh in your life every day. God has never stopped speaking, as some people would like to say. God's words are still being proclaimed all over the earth, and the Spirit of the Living God is just waiting for people to receive it and walk it out so that He can work with those who do this Word. Do you need a miracle in your life? Start speaking the Word of God out loud, not your own words. Our words tend to perpetuate the awful things that happen to us, rather than change them. God's Word is the solution to every problem that has ever existed. Sickness, financial difficulty, family strife, abuse, business issues, bitterness, and any other personal problem you can think of, along with social dilemmas related to government, poverty, crime, environmental issues, and even the economy is dealt with in the Word of God.

When Joshua came to the wall of Jericho, he did not say to the people of Israel, "Well, here's a wall. We can't get around it, we can't go over it, we can't go through it, we might as well turn back." *No way!* Joshua was not moved by what he saw at all. He knew the Word of the Lord, that God had commanded him to take that city.

And the Lord said to Joshua: "See! I have given Jericho into your hand, its king, and the mighty men of valor. You shall march around the city, all you men of war; you shall go all around the city once. This you shall do six days. And seven priests shall bear seven trumpets of rams' horns before the ark. But the seventh day you shall march around the city seven times, and the priests shall blow the trumpets. It shall come to pass, when they make a long blast with the ram's horn, and when you hear the sound of the trumpet, that all the people shall shout with a great shout; then the wall of the city will fall down flat. And the people shall go up every man straight before him" (Joshua 6:2-5).

God commanded Joshua to see the situation the way the Lord saw it. In essence, God was saying, "Don't look at the wall, Joshua. See it through My eyes. In My eyes it has already fallen and you have the victory. As long as you believe that what I see is true rather than what you see with your natural eyes, you will be My partner in bringing My Word to pass. Just don't get caught up with what you think is impossible, because with Me, all things are possible."

Whatever you are facing in your life right now, I promise you that by believing the Word of God you can transform your circumstances. Put down what you see, and hold on to what God sees. Put down what you know, and open up your mind to the thoughts of God! When we decide that the Word of God is a greater reality than even the physical reality we live in, we will have opened the door to allow the Spirit of God to become one with His Word, thus allowing the Word to become flesh in our lives.

John says in his Gospel that when the Word of God becomes flesh, we will behold His glory, the glory as of the only begotten of the Father, full of grace and truth. Within this revelation is the key to seeing the lame walk, the leper cleansed, and the dead man alive. Allowing God's Word to become flesh in your life is the key to seeing a useless hip socket grow a brand-new leg or a dangling wrist joint grow a new hand! Do you believe this can happen? Well, whether you do or not, God believes it and I choose to stand with Him!

Heaven and earth will pass away, but My words will by no means pass away (Mark 13:31).

My covenant I will not break, nor alter the word that has gone out of My lips (Psalm 89:34).

THE SPIRIT UPON THE HEART

*For the eyes of the Lord run to and fro throughout the whole earth, to show Himself strong on behalf of those **whose heart is loyal to Him*** (2 Chronicles 16:9a).

The word "loyal" means a heart like God's. God is looking for a heart just like His. Wherever God finds Himself, there God goes to work. God wants hearts that reflect the power of His Word working through their lives, not unfaithful, fickle lovers who have never allowed the Word to become flesh in their lives! The children of God have got to be trained to hear and obey the Word of the Lord, because only obedience to His will laid out for us in His Word will produce godly fruit in our inner man.

I like what Paul has to say in Second Timothy, "*If we are faithless, He remains faithful; He cannot deny Himself.*" Throughout history, we see how God picked different individuals: David, a man after God's own heart, and Samuel, a man faithful to the heart and mind of God. This intimate working relationship is very important. Let me say it again:

God cannot deny God.

Listen to Jesus' accusation of the Pharisees:

But because I tell the truth, you do not believe Me. Which of you convicts Me of sin? And if I tell the truth, why do you not believe Me? He who is of God hears God's words; therefore you do not hear, because you are not of God (John 8:45-47).

Those who know God, hear His voice. The way His children learn to recognize God's voice is by studying the things He has already said and doing them! I like to say it this way: **The Word of God opens your spiritual ears to hear God.** If we accept God's Word, God will accept us. If we reject God's Word, God will reject us. This is exactly what Samuel told Saul in First Samuel, chapter 15:

But Samuel said to Saul, "I will not return with you, for you have rejected the word of the Lord, and the Lord has rejected you from being king over Israel." And as Samuel turned around to go away, Saul seized the edge of his robe, and it tore. So Samuel said to him, "The Lord has torn the kingdom of Israel from you today, and has given it to a neighbor of yours, who is better than you" (1 Samuel 15:26-28).

Saul showed that he did not reverence, respect, and value the Word of the Lord because he refused to be fully obedient to it. Because he rejected the Word of God, God rejected him. Second Timothy 2:12-13 says:

If we endure, we shall also reign with Him. If we deny Him, He also will deny us. If we are faithless, He remains faithful; He cannot deny Himself.

If we let Him reign, then we shall reign with Him. If we deny Him, He will deny us. If we declare His name before men, He will declare our names before the Father. If we abide in Him, He will abide in us (the Law of Reciprocity)! Jesus teaches us in John 15 that when we abide in God and His Word abides in us, we are in perfect agreement with God. However, if we reject God's Word, we are refusing to receive it. In this situation, it is impossible for God's

Word to abide in us! However, when we abide in God and receive His Word, it will abide in us and produce the fruit of God working with God.

The God we serve is a good farmer. He does not allow His plants to crawl along the ground, underneath the brush, where the sun cannot reach them; plants like that use up nutrients and water from the ground, but they will never produce fruit. In order for a harvest to be produced, the vine must be picked up and tied to a stake or a fence where the sun can strike it with its strong rays. The vine must be pruned, so that those branches that are merely taking up space and not giving anything back, can be trimmed back or totally cut away. Jesus promises in John 15 that God will do the same with us as His children.

> *I am the true vine, and My Father is the vinedresser. Every branch in Me that does not bear fruit He takes away; and every branch that bears fruit He prunes, that it may bear more fruit.* **You are already clean because of the word which I have spoken to you.** *Abide in Me, and I in you. As the branch cannot bear fruit of itself, unless it abides in the vine, neither can you, unless you abide in Me. I am the vine, you are the branches. He who abides in Me, and I in him, bears much fruit; for without Me you can do nothing. If anyone does not abide in Me, he is cast out as a branch and is withered; and they gather them and throw them into the fire, and they are burned.* **If you abide in Me, and My words abide in you, you will ask what you desire, and it shall be done for you.** *By this My Father is glorified, that you bear much fruit; so you will be My disciples* (John 15:1-8).

These verses demonstrate once again that God in you must be in perfect unity with God in Heaven for the fruit of God working with God to be produced in your life.

*When we abide in the intimacy that God has within
Himself, and His Word abides in us, we shall ask for
whatever we desire and it will be done for us.*

If you abide in God and God abides in you, God is in agreement
with God. Then, the answer comes because God is answering His
desire, not yours. Remember, Christ is the Vine, we are the branches. If the branches do not produce, God will prune the branches; if
He cannot work with the branch at all, it is cut off and thrown into
the fire.

In the parable of talents, the Lord took away the talent from the
servant who had received only one, and gave it to the servant with
10 talents. The lazy servant had not respected and reverenced his
Master enough to do something productive with his talent. He had
not even put the talent in the bank so it could gain interest. Because
the servant was unproductive, the Lord cut him off like an unproductive branch. Whatever does not produce will be cut off and
thrown into the fire. The Lord said, "Cast that worthless servant into
outer darkness, where there will be weeping and gnashing of teeth."
This clearly shows that:

What God cannot work with, to hell it goes.

The axe is already laid at the root of the trees; therefore every tree that does not bear good fruit is cut down and thrown into the fire (Matthew 3:10 NASB).

Perhaps this is a harsh reality, but we have to realize something: There is no unsubmitted, rebellious flesh, no unholy emotions or skeptical minds in God's world. In God's reality, there is only God. His plan is to continue to speak His Word over us with an expectation that we will act out His Word until it becomes flesh—thus manifesting the perfect image of God. For this reason, John says in First John 4:17, "*Love has been perfected among us in this: that we may have boldness in the day of judgment; because as He is, so are we in this world.*"

CONCLUSION

Let me just say right now, God is in love with every person reading this book. The truth that He wants to share with you through me is for your freedom not for bondage! I've heard people say, "I want to be godly, but it's just so hard! How can I ever be as holy or as righteous as Jesus was? It's impossible!"

It is a huge blessing for all of us that God says something different. God says that you are the righteousness of God in Christ, that you are seated with Him in heavenly places right now! God wants you to know right now that your destiny is to sit and reign with Him in the Throne of Heaven. You are a son/daughter of God! Your inheritance is everything that God is and everything that He has—He has given it all to you. Now begin to walk in righteousness.

You must remember that God's Word is the key; it is the doorway through which all God's covenant believers must walk in order to experience the fulfillment of the God-destiny that He has for you.

Your responsibility is to engrave what God says about you on your heart, in your mind, and on the palm of your hand. Your confidence must be in the Word, not in what you see around you! It is God's mighty Word that has the power to transform your world into the image of the Word. The key to bearing fruit in your life is accepting God's Word as true. All things are possible to him who believes! So go ahead; dive deep into His Word and find out that what He says He is also able to bring to pass.

TIMELESS TRUTHS FROM CHAPTER THREE

- The Word of God is God's resumé; it is His vision, purpose, and will.

- A word from God is worth a thousand pictures.

- God can bring to pass only what He finds of Himself inside you.

- When we choose to step into the power of God working with God, we are immediately predestined for success. Only God's Word has no choice but to never fail.

- God only hears Himself.

- Intimacy is the birthplace of miracles.

- God cannot deny God.

- When we abide in the intimacy that God has within Himself, and His Word abides in us, we shall ask for whatever we desire and it will be done for us.

- What God cannot work with, to hell it goes.

ENDNOTES

1. Myles Munroe, *Releasing Your Potential* (Shippensburg, PA: Destiny Image Publishers, 1992), 17.

2. Douglas A. Wheeler, *For the Love of God: A Conceptual Study of the Love of God* (Bossier City, LA: Mended Wings Ministries, 1996), 4.

3. H.W.F. Gesenius, *Gesenius' Hebrew-Chaldee Lexicon to the Old Testament* (Grand Rapids, MI: Baker Book House, 1970), 766.

4. John Gill, "Commentary on Genesis 1:2," *The New John Gill Exposition of the Entire Bible,* accessed on the Internet at: http://www.searchgodsword.org/com/wen/view.cgi?book=ge&chapter=001.

CHAPTER FOUR

Sovereignty

GOD'S MASTERPIECE

O Lord, what is man that You care for him, the son of man that You think of him? (Psalm 144:3 NIV).

THROUGHOUT the years, God has given me many prophetic dreams dealing with the revelation of God working with God. One dream that has helped me fully grasp the working relationship that man has with his Creator focused on an oyster in the ocean. In this dream, I saw myself swimming deeper and deeper into the ocean. As I approached the ocean floor, I noticed that it was covered with little objects, which, as I drew closer, I discovered were oysters. Inside one of the oysters was a pearl.

Immediately, when I saw the oyster and the pearl within it, I heard the voice of God say, "It is interesting the way a pearl is made." Perhaps you know that a pearl is formed when a small grain of sand gets inside the oyster. The minuscule, foreign object causes the oyster much irritation; therefore, it secretes a substance that causes the grain of sand to become a pearl.

Upon further investigation after the dream, I found out that, for a pearl to be formed, the grain of sand has to work its way into the lining of the oyster, in order for it to cause enough irritation. When it does, the oyster will envelope the grain of sand in a sac, and it will continue to cover it with hundreds of layers of pearl. Eventually, the pearl will have developed into a beautiful, round object.

Perhaps this is obvious to you, but if I had taken that little oyster out of the ocean and put it in a water jar by my kitchen sink, it would live. It would never again, however, produce a pearl. The process of creating a pearl takes a grain of sand that comes from the ocean floor.

In like manner if we took all of the oysters in the Atlantic Ocean and put them in a huge aquarium in Florida, divers would never again discover a pearl lying docilely on the bottom of the ocean floor. Without the oyster, it is impossible for the ocean to make a pearl. The two are in relationship with each other to produce something neither could make on their own.

It is amazing to me how nature is continually letting the glory of the only true God shine through it so that we may recognize the One who created it and worship His Majesty! The story of the oyster demonstrates to us again the principle of God working with God. In order for an oyster to produce a pearl, it must get some of the ocean sand inside of it. The oyster cannot produce the pearl without sand from the ocean's bottom slipping through and causing great irritation to the oyster. It is the same with God and His children. In order for God to produce pearls of great price (His results) in our lives, He must plant something of Himself inside of us, with which He can work. In this lies a great revelation:

God only works with the God-seed He sows.

Remember, Jesus taught us that anything not birthed in God will be uprooted.

But He answered and said, "Every plant which My heavenly Father has not planted will be uprooted" (Matthew 15:13).

God chooses to reveal Himself in Scripture by using different names for Himself. I normally think about it as the 12 revelations of the name of God. In the first chapter of Genesis, the Hebrew word used for God is *Elohim.*

This is a fascinating word because of what it implied to the original audience of Genesis, the second generation of Israelites who had come out of Egypt. The Hebrew children had become acquainted with many different gods and goddesses while they were in Egypt for 450 years. Most of these gods and goddesses were supposedly spiritual manifestations of the physical world around them. For example, the Egyptians worshiped gods associated with the Nile River and with the sun and moon. Yet when the Israelites were escorted out of that country of bondage by the man of God, Moses, they experienced the true and living God, who claimed to be the exact opposite of the gods and goddesses of Egypt. He was not part of creation; He was above it!

In fact, His Word made every living thing. Even the rocks, rivers, oceans, and mountains came into existence through the Word. The revelatory name used to describe God in Genesis 1 is actually a plural word; *Elohim* can be translated "gods" or "divine beings." The biblical author was trying to make a point to the children of Israel. In essence, Moses was saying, "Our God is not just one among many gods; He is the God of gods, and the Lord of all lords." Moses tied the name YHWH to Elohim in the second chapter of Genesis, calling Him the Lord God. By doing that, Moses was saying that our Elohim was also the Creator and the sovereign God over all creation. With the revelation of this name came the understanding of the plurality of majesty, and it is a sign of esteem rather than an indication of more than one god.

After Elohim had created all of the natural world, the birds and the land animals, the fish and all the sea creatures, the Scripture says that He took a different approach to creating His masterpiece. God came face to face with His creation again. His method for creating the man, Adam, was to form him through the council of His Word and with His hands from the dust of the earth.

> Then God said, "Let Us make man in Our image, according to Our likeness; let them have dominion over the fish of the sea, over the birds of the air, and over the cattle, over all the earth and over every creeping thing that creeps on the earth" (Genesis 1:26).

The Hebrew text in this passage is very rich with meaning. God says, "Let Us make…." The Hebrew word used for "make" is *asah*, which means "to do or make." This word, according to the Vine's Expository Dictionary, is not a strong enough word to connote creation; rather it is the same word used in other places in the Hebrew Scriptures where man is doing and making from already created things. For the creation of man to be uniquely demonstrative of God's creative power, there must be a connection in the Scripture to the word *bara*, which is used only when God creates something. In the very next verse we see that these words are being used interchangeably. Genesis 1:27 says, "*So God created* [bara] *man in His own image; in the image of God He created him; male and female He creat-ed them."* Likewise, Genesis 2:4 states:

> *This the history of the heavens and the earth when they were created* [bara], *in the day that the Lord God made* [asah] *the earth and the heavens.*

The way these words are used interchangeably in these passages is significant. For me it draws a picture in my mind, not of God merely speaking and all things just appearing, though this did happen. I see God down on His hands and knees in the red earth of His creation molding and pounding, slapping the clay around until it became the perfect image that He wanted.

On a side note, looking at creation in this light should help us to understand the importance of taking care of our bodies. *Our anatomy is God's most complete biography of Himself!* We should honor God by giving up habits that destroy our physical self, allowing the Holy Spirit to give us the strength to discipline and buffet our bodies for the sake of the Word of God, the Gospel of Jesus Christ.

The next important picture I want you to see is found in the words, "Then God said." Up until this point, every word that God spoke caused something to take place immediately. God said, "Let there be light." And there was light. Until verse 26, the Scripture does not imply that any long time periods took place while God "performed" what He had said. According to Genesis 1, there had been merely a five-day period in which God spoke all things into existence, including the length and form of those days. With the creation of man, we encounter God having a conversation. He says, "Let Us create man in Our own image." It seems that God is having a conversation with Himself; He is holding council within His own will, and amazingly enough, everyone agrees! There is no fighting, not even a light discussion. God is in agreement with His own Word.

This whole process sets man apart as special above all of creation. He is not like the animals, the plants, and the rivers. He is a separate entity, which was created to have dominion over all these things. Though he is a created being, man will receive from God His own Spirit, His mind, will, and emotions, and the perfection of God's working relationship with Himself. God will make man a master copy of Himself, without flaw or blemish—His own son in every way. God takes council within Himself to form for Himself a son. God spoke to Himself.

A PICTURE OF THE CREATION OF MAN

The mist was lying cool on all the plants of the garden that day. God came and walked among them, as the animals gathered to Him to see what He would say. The sun was low on the horizon, not a sound could be heard but the gentle bubble of water from the nearby river. Then God bent down. Slowly and gently, He put His mighty knees on the grass, and all the animals lay down peacefully around Him. The Mighty God leaned over, until His nose was hovering over the dew-covered grass, and breathed deeply. As He exhaled, the sound of His Spirit could be heard on the distant mountains, and all around Him little daisies sprang up from the ground. He chuckled low and winked at a jackrabbit, staring at Him from the edge of the trees. What was God going to do next?

It seemed that the whole earth was sleeping. Then God let His large hands drop in front of Him. His hands pressed through the grass and deep into the red earth of the garden floor. God pulled out a clump of clay and set it next to Him. He repeated this action until He had made quite a large pile of red earth to His right side. Then He stood up and looked carefully at the pile of dirt. Again,

He gently dropped to His knees and dug His great big hands into the pile of dirt. God was molding something.

As the object took form in front of God, the animals looked on in amazement. The red dirt, from which God was receiving so much pleasure as He formed it with His hands, was taking on the shape of someone the animals knew. It was a sculpture of God Himself! Out of His belly came a low and gentle laugh again, as if He was so pleased. Now He held the statue up and looked at it from head to toe. He picked up the God-image and held it close to Him. He placed His large mouth right on top of the sculpture's mouth and breathed deeply.

As He exhaled, the sound of His Spirit echoed on the canyon walls and rustled the leaves of the mighty Cyprus trees. The image of God held tightly in God's mighty hands began to move, as its lungs breathed in the breath of God and accepted the life of the Father. God looked around the garden at the trees and animals and said, "Now he is a man. He is My image. He is My son." And God and the man walked and talked in the garden that day and had perfect communion with each other.

As God formed man with His hands and breathed into him His own life-breath, this new creation became Adam.

A GODLIKE TASK

After God created Adam, He rested. I can just imagine God and Adam lying in a field looking up at the clouds, laughing together, as God tells Adam of His plans and teaches him of His glory. Nothing hinders Adam from receiving God's love, because the man is fully convinced that God is his Father, that Adam has his Father's attention and approval; this God-man is in full obedience to God. Since man was created to imitate God in all things (Ephesians 5:1 [NASB] says, "*Therefore be imitators of God, as beloved children*"), then naturally, Adam was called to do and make just as God had done. So it was natural for God to give Adam a creative responsibility. God decides that Adam will name the animals.

> *Out of the ground the Lord formed every beast of the field and bird of the air, and brought them to Adam to see what he would call them. And whatever Adam called each living creature, that was its name* (Genesis 2:19).

Can you see a picture in your mind of God leading each individual animal to Adam so that the man could name them? This idea clearly demonstrates to us the working relationship that God had with His son Adam. The biblical author is trying to convey the truth that God was in a covenant relationship with Adam. God gave Adam the responsibility of naming all of the animals. The process of picking names for the animals may not seem overly important in modern terms, but to the ancient readers of Genesis, this would have had great implications.

In antiquity, the name of a person or place was tied to its destiny in relationship to the covenantal people of God. For example, let us look at Abraham, the Father of the Jewish nation. This man was named Abram by his parents, which means in Hebrew, "high father," according to the New Strong's Expanded Dictionary of the Words in the Hebrew Bible.[1] Yet God chose to change his name to Abraham when He came into covenant relationship with YHWH. *Abraham* means "father of a multitude" in Hebrew.[2] The reason Abraham was given this name was as a means of speaking those things which aren't as though they are. Paul claims in Romans 4:17, that our God is the One who calls those things that are not as though they were, and that is exactly what God did with Abraham. God gave Abraham this name with the expectation that Abraham would have thousands of children, even though, at the time, he had none. We see that God's word did not fail, for Abraham did become the father of a mighty nation; now his descendants are as numerous as the sand by the seashore.

The importance of names carries on throughout the history of the children of Israel. After Sarah's death, Abraham took a new wife, named Keturah. She had six sons, whom Abraham sent to the east of Canaan away from his son Isaac, to whom Abraham gave all of his possessions. One of the sons of Keturah was named Midian. Well, we all know who the Midianites are! From this line came the wife of Moses, and in the days of Gideon, the Midianites terrorized the children of Israel until Gideon's army of 300 men destroyed them. By the way, the name *Midian* means "brawling and contention" (Strong's Hebrew Dictionary)! Is it not intriguing that Midian was used by God as a source of strife and contention because of the Israelite's disobedience to God during the reign of the judges? We see clearly that God and His people have special names that indicate their nature and character.

The word for "name" in Hebrew is *shem*, and it connotes a sense of destiny, individuality, character, renown, or reputation. Can you see how God used Adam to release the God-destiny of each animal? From my personal study, I am convinced that when the animals were brought to Adam, they all had a similar appearance, substance, and form. It was not until Adam actually named the animals that he gave them their shape and individuality. God used Adam's mouth to speak a destiny that had not yet been spoken.

This awesome working relationship that we see demonstrated by God and Adam can help bring clarity to the issue of God's sovereignty. Many people ask, "How can God be sovereign and man still have a free will?" We must remember that our origin is in God. Unlike all the animals Adam named, we are made like God. We were created to be in a partnership with Him, not far off or distanced by sin and iniquity; nor were we created to be slaves. We are sons and daughters of God, and ambassadors of the King of kings. God wants to rule and reign in sovereignty through us!

The Word of God teaches us that it is impossible for two to walk together unless they agree. God is not going to be unequally yoked together with unbelievers. In order for Adam to "speak those things that are not as though they were," the man would have to be in perfect agreement with the Father, just as Jesus walked in perfect agreement with the Father during His earthly ministry. Philippians says:

Let this mind be in you which was also in Christ Jesus, who, being in the form of God, did not consider it robbery to be equal with God (Philippians 2:5-6).

In the same way, God has given us the mind of Christ so that we can walk in perfect agreement with Him. Jesus said in Matthew 18:20, "*For where two or three are gathered in My name, I am there in the midst of them.*"

We have to realize that when we come together in agreement, I am in His name and you are in His name. Agreement in the Spirit is that God in me is in agreement with God in you. *God works with us to the degree that we harmonize with His will.*

*I'm in the name and you're in the name—
God is in our midst.*

GOD CANNOT LIE

In His sovereignty, God has chosen to bind His will and the subsequent actions He takes to His Word. There are a few places in the Hebrew Scriptures where God is quoted as saying, "I repent for...." However, the phrase, "I'm just kidding," is not spoken even one time by God. God has never gone back and changed what He said. For example, in Genesis 1, God says, "*Let Us make man in Our own image....*" In Genesis 6:6, Moses says, "*The Lord was sorry that He had made man on the earth, and He was grieved in His heart.*" Amazingly, God regretted that He had made man. Perhaps we would expect God to, in His wrath, proclaim, "Man is no longer My image bearer!" Yet remember that God cannot change His Word. Instead, He reinforces the truth of man's true identity in Genesis 9:6: "*Whoever sheds man's blood, by man his blood shall be shed; for in the image of God He made man.*" Even though God repented forever having created man, He still would not go back on His original Word, that man was created to bear the image of the Most High God.

It is important to see that God is bound by covenant relationship to keep His Word. When the Israelites rejected the Word of the Lord and built a golden calf, there was only one thing standing between them and God's wrath: Moses and his relationship with God. Because of Moses, God kept His Word and did not harm the children of Israel, even though they deserved His judgment.

This is not the only Scripture that demonstrates how seriously God takes His Word. Titus 1:2 says: "*in hope of eternal life which **God, who cannot lie,** promised before time began.*"

Hebrews 6:18 also states "*that by two immutable things, in which it is **impossible for God to lie**, we might have strong consolation, who have fled for refuge to lay hold of the hope set before us.*"

Here it is twice in the most simple terms: God cannot lie! Obviously the fact that God opened His mouth and spoke, "Let there be light," in Genesis chapter 1, and light immediately came into existence, shows explicitly that God could never prove false in anything. His words carry within them the power to come to pass. Every time He speaks, it becomes fact! You have to know that nothing will ever come out of God except that which is already inside of Him. His Word and His Spirit agree because the Word and God are one. Even within the realm of human relationships we see the same principle at work. To know what is in a person, we have to listen to their words. Their words show us what they are made of.

For out of the abundance of the heart the mouth speaks (Matthew 12:34; see also Luke 6:45).

Jesus is not kidding around with the power of the tongue here. The tongue and the heart will always be in agreement with each other. I have encountered people where this truth is painfully obvious. Have you ever had a discussion with a person who is afraid of many things? Is it not interesting that everything they say centers around fear?

For example, in the line at the grocery store a lady says, "Did you see the weather report this morning? They said there might be a thunderstorm. I'm afraid it might damage my petunias!"

Another person pipes in and says, "That's right! Do you remember that huge storm last July? The hail from it destroyed almost all of my perennials. This year I'm not taking any chances. I bought one of those big weather resistant tarps to put over my bushes."

The first lady responds, "Yes, I bet it will rip right through my property. I'm afraid I'm not very well prepared for storms. What if lightning hits? I watched a story on TV just recently about a woman whose barn was burned down because of a lightning strike. Big storms scare me because they are so unpredictable!"

Do you see how her heart is showing in her words? Just from these few sentences, we can see that she is expecting the worst—and is woefully unprepared to handle her worst-case scenario! She is afraid her plants will be killed, her land damaged, and her buildings burnt down. She is afraid of unpredictable circumstances, and she is terrified of lightning. She is nervous because she has no plan of action in case hail hits, and she is nervous about what the other woman in the grocery line thinks of her because of her lack of preparation! This woman is a real worrywart! The fear that is in her heart is painfully obvious to you and me because of her words. Her fear is affecting her whole way of life, and anyone with a little discernment can see it.

Even though this woman is not trying to expose her deepest secrets, her mouth will always agree with her heart. In this way, God's image is still operating through mankind. God is the fully transparent One. He has nothing to hide. His words and His heart are always in agreement. Unlike God, however, not everything that comes out of a man's heart is good. Jesus' reply to the Pharisees showed that their religious words and the traditions of men openly exposed them:

> *You are of your father the devil, and the desires of your father you want to do. He was a murderer from the beginning, and does not stand in the truth, because there is no truth in him. When he speaks a lie, he speaks from his own resources, for he is a liar and the father of it* (John 8:44).

Jesus proclaims that within the devil there is no truth, for out of his own resources he speaks lies. The devil is procedurally doing the same thing as God: God speaks and acts out of the overflow of His own heart; and in the same manner, the devil is operating out of the substance of who he is. He has rejected being in partnership with God, or in any way working with God. The devil has no tools except what lies within his own fallen nature. He, the devil, has been cut off from God's creative words, all that is left in him is lies.

In many ways in Scripture it appears that satan was given permission to do what he does best and that is to kill, steal, and destroy. It may seem hard to believe, but God sovereignly permits the devil to work with sin even in His own children. Remember satan is bound to the realms of darkness.

Let us look at Isaiah 55:11 again. Try to visualize the God-working-with-God relationship between the Father and His Word.

> *So shall My Word be that goes forth from My mouth; it shall not return to Me void, but it shall accomplish what I please, and it shall prosper in the thing for which I sent it* (Isaiah 55:11).

The principle we see demonstrated in the above Scripture is this: God's Word is God's will. God is working to bring His Word to pass so that His will can be accomplished.

∽∽∼

Without the fulfillment of God's Word,
His will can never be brought to fruition.

∽∽∼

Man's role in the fulfillment of God is his ability to choose whether or not he will be involved with it at all—man does not therefore control the outcome! God can and will find other people to work through if we refuse to conform to His image. The anchor that we hold to is not tossed to and fro by the whims of men; no, it is steadfastly set within the Holy of Holies, where all of God's promises are *Yes* and *Amen*.

Our job as children of God is to continually accept God's Word as truth and allow God to bring it to pass in our lives. The process of yielding to the creative flow within God's Word is a strategic key to unlocking God's dynamite power, which He predetermined to flow through those who decide to yield their will to His. In this, God's sovereignty is perfectly demonstrated. The idea is that by allowing the Word of God to become flesh in our lives, we as children of God will actually become the will of God. As we take on God's form, His substance, His essence, we will stop "doing" and "being obedient to" God's will, and actually become His will, and thus manifest God's Kingdom on earth. Do you remember what Jesus said in Revelation?

> *He who overcomes, I will make him a pillar in the temple of My God, and he shall go out no more. I will write on him the name of My God and the name of the city of My God, the New Jerusalem, which comes down out of heaven from My God. And I will write on him My new name. ...Behold I stand at the door and knock. If anyone hears My voice and opens the door, I will come in to him and dine with him, and he with Me* (Revelation 3:12,20).

What is Jesus clearly conveying to the churches? "If you will hear My voice, and open the door to Me, then I will write on you the name of My God, My own name, and the name of the city of My God. When self-will and self-desire are swallowed up in passion for Me, then you and I will become one. Your name will no longer be important to you, because your eyes will be opened to see that it is in Me that you live, move, and have your being. You will take on My image, My name, My authority. What I am, you will be; what I say, you will say; and what I do, you will be equipped to do. In this John the Baptist spoke correctly, 'He must increase; but I must decrease.' All you are will be swallowed up in all that I am."

God's sovereign will, His power, glory, knowledge, wisdom, beauty, understanding, foreknowledge, and truth will now be perfectly demonstrated to the whole universe through men, women, and children—those who have completely died to self and are now fully living in and through God. The Book of John, chapter 1, shows us this so well. Let's look again at this passage:

In the beginning was the Word, and the Word was with God, and the Word was God. He was in the beginning with God. All things were made through Him, and without Him nothing was made that was made. …He came to His own, and His own did not receive Him. But as many as received Him, to them He gave the right to become children of God, to those who believe in His name: who were born, not of blood, nor of the will of the flesh, nor of the will of man, but of God (John 1:1-3, 11-13).

Do you see that God wants to do with us the exact same procedure He did to bring the God-man Jesus into existence? These verses prove it! *"The Word became flesh and dwelt among us,"* John 1:14 says, *"and we beheld His glory, the glory as of the only begotten of the Father, full of grace and truth."* In the same manner God wants us to receive the God-seed, His Word, into our lives. He wants to work diligently with His Word to bring it to completion in our lives.

If we receive the seed of God, we have learned there is but one thing that seed can produce: It must produce after its own kind. It must produce God! God-seeds produce God results. We also have to realize that God is sovereign! God is only bound to do what His own nature and character say He must do. We have to realize that God will judge us by bringing to pass every negative and harmful thing we say. In this way, God responded to the children of Israel in Numbers 14:28: *"Say to them, 'As I live,' says the Lord, 'just as you have spoken in My hearing, so I will do to you....'"* His Word, as Hebrews chapter 1 says, is His express image. It is a perfect picture of what God is through and through. We have to realize that God is driven to bring Himself to pass. But if His children will not willingly conform to His Word, God's judgment will then expose sin. If the plan that God has for your life is not coming to pass, there must be areas of your life that you are not allowing God to renew and transform by His Word.

At this point I would like to clarify what God's sovereignty is not. Some people may think that if God is really all-powerful, then He can do anything, whether good or bad. This is not true. The reason: God cannot do anything that is contrary to His essence, His nature, and character. For example, God could never choose to die. Though the Scripture says He holds the measure of man's days in His hand, to bless them with long life or to wipe out the remembrance of them forever, yet He can never die. He is the eternal, self-existing One. There is no death in God.

God cannot go against His Word. God cannot lie. God cannot abide with the wicked, nor can an evil man approach God. God cannot forgive sins without the shedding of blood! God cannot break covenant. And how do we know that God cannot do these things? Because His Word says He cannot. The Holy Scriptures are a testimony of God, and they teach that God has chosen to bind His ability to choose by His own character. God's sovereignty is therefore unlimited in goodness, love, holiness, justice, righteousness, kindness, compassion, judgment, truth, and light; His power is unlimited to bring His nature and character to pass, not a corrupt nature.

Many people have a warped view of God's sovereignty because they blame Him for circumstances in their life that were caused by disobedience to God. When we come into a covenant with God, we are saying that we will also be bound to God's nature and character, not our own. The concept of covenant says that both parties are required to keep certain laws and codes, which are usually set down by the stronger party. In other words, God writes out the contract, and the only real choice we have is whether or not we will sign it. We don't get to decide what is in the contract. When we come to the table with God, we come empty handed. We have nothing to offer God, because He is the Master of all things. God's contract is His Word.

Here are some examples of God's covenant straight from the Scriptures:

But what does it say? "The word is near you, in your mouth and in your heart" (that is, the word of faith which we preach): that if you confess with your mouth the Lord Jesus and believe in your heart that God has raised Him from the dead, you will be saved (Romans 10:8-9).

Therefore submit to God. Resist the devil and he will flee from you. Draw near to God and He will draw near to you. Cleanse your hands, you sinners; and purify your hearts, you double-minded. Lament and mourn and weep! Let your laughter be turned to mourning and your joy to gloom. Humble yourselves in the sight of the Lord, and He will lift you up (James 4:7-10).

Ask, and it will be given to you; seek, and you will find; knock, and it will be opened to you. For everyone who asks receives, and he who seeks finds, and to him who knocks it will be opened. Or what man is there among you who, if his son asks for bread, will give him a stone? Or if he asks for a fish, will he give him a serpent? If you then, being evil, know how to give good gifts to your children, how much more will your Father who is in heaven give good things to those who ask Him! Therefore, whatever you want men to do to you, do also to them, for this is the Law and the Prophets (Matthew 7:7-12).

God's Word makes it clear—there is only one Way to come into relationship with God, and that Way is Jesus. God's sovereignty says, "Once you come into covenant with Me, you become My property, not your own. If you call Me Lord, then I will possess what is Mine." When the Word of God comes out of your mouth, God hears Himself and responds: SAVED!! God is His Word; He is bound by His own character to perform it. Clearly, our only choice is to believe God's Word and come into covenant with Him both in words spoken and action.

GOD SWEARS BY HIMSELF

My covenant I will not break, nor alter the word that has gone out of My lips (Psalm 89:34).

...and said: "By Myself I have sworn, says the Lord, because you have done this thing, and have not withheld your son, your only son—blessing I will bless you, and multiplying I will multiply your descendants as the stars of the heaven and as the sand which is on the seashore; and your descendants shall possess the gates of their enemies" (Genesis 22:16-17).

God subjects Himself to Himself.

God has sworn by Himself, and He, like anyone else, is only as good as His Word. God wants us to remind Him of what He has already said. Think about the parable of the friend who came knocking for bread in the middle of the night.

And He said to them, "Which of you shall have a friend, and go to him at midnight and say to him, 'Friend, lend me three loaves; for a friend of mine has come to me on his journey, and I have nothing to set before him'; and he will answer from within and say, 'Do not trouble me; the door is now shut, and my children are with me in bed; I cannot rise and give to you'? I say to you, though he will not rise and give to him because he is his friend, yet because of his persistence he will rise and give him as many as he needs (Luke 11:5-8).

Then He spoke a parable to them, that men always ought to pray and not lose heart, saying: "There was in a certain city a judge who did not fear God nor regard man. Now there was a widow in that city; and she came to him, saying, 'Get justice for me from my adversary.' And he would not for a while; but afterward he said within himself, 'Though I do not fear God nor regard man, yet because this widow troubles me I will avenge her, lest by her continual coming she weary me.'" Then the Lord said, "Hear what the unjust judge said. And shall God not avenge His own elect who cry out day and night to Him, though He bears long with them? I tell you that He will avenge them speedily" (Luke 18:1-8a).

These two passages amaze me! They definitely go against the usual religious status quo about God's attitude toward prayer. After all, God knows what we have need of before we ask, true? Then why do we need to show God persistence and perseverance when it comes to making our requests known? Remember, God's integrity is wrapped up in whether or not He keeps His Word. Can you imagine your dad on earth saying to you, "I have sworn by myself—I will take you out for ice cream if you are faithful to finish your homework. Yet if you do not finish your homework, I will administer the rod of correction." Not only that, Dad says, "Furthermore, I expect you to continually remind me of the promise I have made. Do not let me forget, for I have sworn by myself, and I will not break my word!" Yet this is exactly how God portrays Himself in His Word.

Do you know that God does not believe in good intentions? Integrity and reputation are based in being a promise keeper; keeping your word gives you a good name with your family your friends and the world. God through His Word created this principle.

I have sworn by myself, the word has gone out of My mouth in righteousness, and shall not return, that to Me every knee shall bow, every tongue shall take an oath (Isaiah 45:23).

"But if you will not hear these words, I swear by Myself," says the Lord, *"that this house shall become a desolation"* (Jeremiah 22:5).

It is as if God were saying, "If I don't do it, then I am not who I say I am! If I don't do it, then I'll give up My throne and you can be god!" Once God swears by Himself it is as good as done.

In history if a document was sealed by the king's signet ring, that document carried authority in every land where that man was king. Think of the story of Esther. Once the king of Persia had decreed that all Jews were to be killed, not even the king could change that law! Instead, the king had to decree that the Jews could defend themselves against their attackers, which the king had decreed to attack them! Once the king had spoken, no one could change his word.

Though these kings were fallible and full of corruption, in this way they were mimicking God and the power of His Word. When

God swears by Himself, He is decreeing a thing by His own omniscience, omnipotence, and omnipresence. He is releasing Himself, His Word, to accomplish the thing that He sent it for.

The Lord God has sworn by His holiness: "Behold, the days shall come upon you when He will take you away with fishhooks, and your posterity with fishhooks" (Amos 4:2).

Do you know that circa 722 B.C., the Northern Kingdom of Israel, whose capital city was Samaria, fell to the Assyrians? It is a well-documented historical fact, also, that the Assyrians carried away their prisoners with large hooks through the nose; therefore the Lord kept His Word and punished the Israelites for their godless abominations. Interestingly enough, though God sent many prophets to the children of Israel pleading with them that they should turn from their wickedness, God also sovereignly knew that they would not repent, and therefore prophesied their inevitable punishment.

I can sense urgency in the spirit that requires us to have a more explicit understanding of God's sovereignty, which is being caused by a shift—a fast-moving transition happening right now in the earth. When we fully grasp how God's sovereignty is actually bound to His Word, we will see that understanding it is a key to unlocking the workings of God in our life. When we realize that God is just looking for people who are willing to receive God's utterances, to bring His Word to pass in our lives, we will see how simple it can be to totally yield ourselves to His plan, purpose, and vision for our lives. We must receive the seed of God's Word and allow the Holy Spirit to go to work with that Word, in order for God's will to manifest in our lives. We must allow a working relationship to be established between God's Word and His Spirit in our very beings. In this way, we can step into the accomplishment of all that God is and all that He has spoken. His sovereignty will be effectively working in and through us.

The Spirit and the Word

Within the Godhead, there is perfect unity and interdependency; the Father, the Word, and the Holy Spirit. It is evident through the Scriptures that God has no needs, except the obvious, that He needs Himself! The Three are in perfect agreement to accomplish the will of God; they do not have separate thoughts, ideas, or wills. As Jesus clearly explains to us in John 5:19-21:

Most assuredly, I say to you, the Son can do nothing of Himself, but what He sees the Father do; for whatever He does, the Son also does in like manner. For the Father loves the Son, and shows Him all things that He Himself does; and He will show Him greater works than these, that you may marvel. For as the Father raises the dead and gives life to them, even so the Son gives life to whom He will.

Here we see demonstrated the working relationship between God the Father and God the Son. We also know that Jesus was filled with the Holy Spirit; therefore, all three are at work here, the Spirit being the agent by which Jesus is in communication with His Father. This beautiful relationship reminds me of another passage, where three men were in unity, working together to accomplish a common goal. The story is found in Exodus, chapter 17.

Now Amalek came and fought with Israel in Rephidim. And Moses said to Joshua, "Choose us some men and go out, fight with Amalek. Tomorrow I will stand on the top of the hill with the rod of God in my hand." So Joshua did as Moses said to him, and fought with Amalek. And Moses, Aaron, and Hur went up to the top of the hill. And so it was, when Moses held up his hand, that Israel prevailed; and when he let down his hand, Amalek prevailed. But Moses' hands became heavy; so they took a stone and put it under him, and he sat on it. And Aaron and Hur supported his hands, one on one side, and the other on the other side; and his hands were steady until the going down of the sun. So Joshua defeated Amalek and his people with the edge of the sword (Exodus 17:8-13).

In order for Israel to prevail against the Amalekites, Moses needed the assistance of his two friends, Aaron and Hur. They lifted the arms of their leader high above their enemy. I believe strongly that when the Spirit of God goes to work with the Word of God, this is when God is truly exalted; for Jesus said, *"I only say what I hear My Father saying; I only do what I see My Father doing."* The revelation of God working with God will always bring God to the forefront—not us! It will always cause glory and honor and praise to come to God. As Aaron and Hur lifted up the arms of Moses in the wilderness, and the children of Israel were victorious over their enemies, so the working relationship between the Spirit and the Word will lift up and exalt God, so that a supernatural explosion of God's glory will cause divine interventions and huge victories over our enemies!

For there are three that bear witness in heaven: the Father, the Word, and the Holy Spirit; and these three are one. And there are three that bear witness on earth: the Spirit, the water, and the blood; and these three agree as one (1 John 5:7-8).

Again, these verses demonstrate the working relationship between God the Father, the Word, and the Spirit. They are in perfect agreement with one another. These are the three who sat in council together at the beginning of all things to create an image bearer called man, who demonstrated fully the fundamental principle within the Godhead of complete unity and wholeness. Creating them male and female demonstrated the plurality of the Godhead and His diversity in essence. It was these three unified as one who visited Abraham and sat with him underneath the tree, who allowed

Abraham to take part in council concerning the action to be taken toward Sodom and Gomorrah, as the friend of God. It is these three who were all present on the day that Jesus, the Living Word, was baptized in the Jordan by John. As the Holy Spirit descended on Jesus in the form of a dove, the Father spoke from Heaven and declared, "*This is My beloved Son, in whom I am well pleased.*" What a glorious painting of God's greatness we can see when we view Him through the revelation of the covenant relationship between the Father, the Word, and the Spirit. Again and again the Spirit and the Word are mentioned together, as the Father speaks, revealing Himself to men.

THE SPIRIT, THE WORD, THE TONGUE

The Spirit of the Lord God spoke by me, and His word was on my tongue (2 Samuel 23:2).

Turn at my rebuke; surely I will pour out my spirit on you; I will make my words known to you (Proverbs 1:23).

James teaches us that the tongue is like the rudder of a ship. Large ships can be turned and swayed by such a small device as a rudder. In the same manner, the tongue is the rudder of the body; the words that we speak are the direction in which we will head. In this way we imitate God and His Word, because God is continually seeing His Word come to pass. That is why we should meditate on what God says, instead of the filth of the world, so that our words will line up with God. To have a bridled tongue means to have a tongue trained to speak only what it hears the Father saying.

"As for Me," says the Lord, "this is My covenant with them: My Spirit who is upon you, and My words which I have put in your

mouth, shall not depart from your mouth, nor from the mouth of your descendants, nor from the mouth of your descendants' descendants," says the Lord, *"from this time and forevermore"* (Isaiah 59:21).

Why is it that God stresses the importance of the Word of God being in our mouths? Perhaps some people would say, "If God says it, isn't that enough?" I tell you the truth; it is only enough if we know that it is God's Word, which He has placed in our mouths! Proclaiming the truth of what God says so that our circumstances line up with the Word is our responsibility as children of God. It was the Word of God in Peter's mouth that caused Tabitha to stand up alive from the dead when Peter said, "Tabitha, arise."

At Joppa there was a certain disciple named Tabitha, which is translated Dorcas. This woman was full of good works and charitable deeds which she did. But it happened in those days that she became sick and died. When they had washed her, they laid her in an upper room. And since Lydda was near Joppa, and the disciples had heard that Peter was there, they sent two men to him, imploring him not to delay in coming to them. Then Peter arose and went with them. When he had come, they brought him to the upper room. And all the widows stood by him weeping, showing the tunics and garments which Dorcas had made while she was with them. But Peter put them all out, and knelt down and prayed. And turning to the body he said, "Tabitha, arise." And she opened her eyes, and when she saw Peter she sat up (Acts 9:36-40).

This story fascinates me. Here is a man named Peter. This man had seen dead people come alive before, through the ministry of Jesus, and perhaps he had also raised someone from the dead before this. When Jesus sent out the 12 in Matthew 10, He commanded them to *"heal the sick, cleanse the leper, raise the dead...."* It is not recorded for us to know if Peter actually did that; however, we do know that he was greatly exposed to God's power to overcome death. Why, he even saw Jesus resurrected from the dead.

If he was just going on past experiences, Peter had no reason to doubt that God would raise this woman from the dead. In fact, bringing her back to life would probably seem like the natural thing to do in Peter's case. The question might arise, however, about how God's sovereignty plays a part in this story. Was it God's will for her to die or not? If it was His will for her to die, why then did Peter raise her to life again? If it was not God's will for her to die, why did it happen in the first place?

The first fact I would like to point out is in regard to the details of Tabitha's life mentioned in the story. Verse 36 says that she was a disciple, full of good works and charitable deeds. In other words, Tabitha was a Christian, a child of God, who had a servant's heart and helped others freely. We are later told that she actually made clothes for the poor and destitute. Here we have a woman who, because of her encounter with Jesus Christ that led her to salvation, was walking out the love of the Father toward the people around her. Obviously, the God-working-with-God principle of "give and it shall be given unto you" applies here, along with the truth that "whatever you sow," according to Galatians 6:7, "*you shall also reap.*" "*Whoever sows to the Spirit,*" Paul says, "*will reap in the Spirit.*"

If there were such a thing as a God-working-with-God account, this woman's would be full! So when she was attacked by death, God would not allow death to hold her. God rescued what He saw of Himself within Tabitha from the power of death. God allowed the woman to be touched merely so that He could show Himself mighty by accomplishing His Word in and through her. Her testimony, we are told later in the chapter, caused many to be saved in that region. God's sovereign will was that His Word would come to pass, that His power and character would be demonstrated, and that the effect would be that people would receive the word of salvation and come into the Kingdom.

When we allow the Spirit of God within us to work with the Word of God in our mouths, we will begin to raise people from the dead, walk on water, and tell the sun and moon to stand still, and it will be done for us by our Father who is in Heaven.

So he answered and said to me: "This is the word of the Lord to Zerubbabel: 'Not by might, nor by power, but by My Spirit,' says the Lord of hosts" (Zechariah 4:6).

Neither can the Word of God be accomplished by philosophies and traditions or formulas created by men that lack basis in the Word. The Word of God will not be brought to pass through the flesh, nor can we be perfected and made like God through the flesh. We have to allow the Spirit of God to work with the Word of God. Only when the two come together in perfect unity will the Word become flesh, and we will behold His glory in our lives—the glory of the only begotten of the Father, full of grace and truth.

Many people seek a prophetic word when they are going through rough times. They need to realize, however, that when the Spirit of God within them is fed the written Word of God, the prophetic word will grow inside of them. Prophecy is merely the Spirit of God upon a specific Word from Scripture that is applicable to a person's circumstances. Prophecy takes the written Word and brings it into the now. If we fill our minds with God's written Word, we will have a prophetic word to encourage ourselves with in any circumstance!

Think of David, when his enemies came against him and even kidnapped his wives and took his city captive in First Samuel 30. What did he do while he was there? The Scripture says that he encouraged himself in the Lord, and the Psalms are a record of what he said.

I will say to God my Rock, "Why have You forgotten me? Why do I go mourning because of the oppression of my enemy?" As with a breaking of my bones, my enemies reproach me, while they say to me all the day long, "Where is your God?" Why are you cast down, O my soul? And why are you disquieted within me? Hope in God; for I shall yet praise Him, the help of my countenance and my God (Psalm 42:9-11).

David prophesied to himself; he spoke the truth of God's Word over his own life. Remember, you are the prophet of your own life. Occasionally God uses others in the Lord to speak the Word to us, but we also need to train and discipline our own mouths with God's Word.

It is the Spirit who gives life; the flesh profits nothing. The words that I speak to you are spirit, and they are life (John 6:63).

And take the helmet of salvation, and the sword of the Spirit, which is the word of God (Ephesians 6:17).

The Word of God is the Spirit's number one weapon! This Scripture creates a picture in my mind of the Person of the Holy Spirit swinging a huge, double-edged sword to slice and dice all of the enemies of God. Remember the Word is not the Sword of Warren Hunter; it is the sword of the Spirit, He has the right to wield this weapon. The Word may come out of my mouth, but it is the Spirit who will direct what I speak like a sword. As it comes out of my mouth it will perform Hebrews 4:12, to cut asunder and divide between bone and marrow, and spirit and soul.

It is as if the Spirit is the great surgeon who knows exactly where to cut in order to reach the tumor or diseased area and cut it out, before it affects the whole body. If I am not yielded to the Spirit, if

I am operating by might and power, instead of by the wisdom of the Spirit of God, I may cut off the patient's left arm, and never even touch the place where the problem is located! First Corinthians says that the Spirit searches the deep things of God and reveals them to us, giving us the Word, which will cut to the heart of the matter and will deal with the issues of the heart, not just the surface symptoms. The Spirit must be within us and the Word in our mouth in order for God's results to take place. The Word inside you has an assignment to a specific person or group that God has for you.

John the beloved disciple paints a powerful picture of the authority of the Word of God in the Book of Revelation:

> *Now I saw heaven opened, and behold, a white horse. And He who sat on him was called Faithful and True, and in righteousness He judges and makes war. His eyes were like a flame of fire, and on His head were many crowns. He had a name written that no one knew except Himself. He was clothed with a robe dipped in blood, and His name is called The Word of God. And the armies in heaven, clothed in fine linen, white and clean, followed Him on white horses. Now out of His mouth goes a sharp sword, that with it He should strike the nations. And He Himself will rule them with a rod of iron. He Himself treads the winepress of the fierceness and wrath of Almighty God* (Revelation 19:11-15).

God has created a standard by which He judges all things—His Word. This is God's sovereignty—not that we escape the personal responsibility of covenant by denying our role in God's plans, but that we have the opportunity to fully yield to the Spirit and the Word, allowing our lives to be agents of God's sovereign will, purpose, plan, design, and vision for all of His creation. God has chosen you, called you, and set you apart from the foundations of the world to be holy and without blame before Him in love. When you recognize the potential of God's Word and allow the Spirit to make the Word flesh in you, you will see that God sovereignly chose you in His will.

Who has saved us and called us with a holy calling, not according to our works, but according to His own purpose and grace which was granted us in Christ Jesus from all eternity (2 Timothy 1:9 NASB).

CONCLUSION

God's sovereignty is a subject that may seem hard to grasp on the outset. I promise, however, that the greater the understanding we have of the power and importance of God's Word in our lives, the less confusing God's sovereignty will be. First, we have to recognize that we are in a divine relationship with God established upon covenant. Remember that covenant is a two-sided contract, in which both parties are expected to keep their promises. We know, according to the Scripture, that God's Word is God's contract with us; it is our guarantee of what we can expect from God.

God is bound by nothing under the sun, except His own nature and character. God chooses to bind Himself to Himself, and as we know, the Word and God are one and the same. If the Word says anything concerning a certain circumstance or issue, we can have confidence that what the Word says is also exactly what God thinks about that circumstance or issue. We can also be sure that what God said about it is true and will not change; rather it will come to pass. God's Word was built for success—it cannot fail, nor can it be altered.

Our role in this covenant is to accept that what God says was not just true for the men and women of the Bible, our grandparents or our farthest-reaching ancestors. In fact, it is true and binding for us today. If we refuse to yield to the Word of His covenant, we will be bound for failure and destruction; if we yield ourselves to the power of the Word of God, and allow the Spirit of God to hover over that Word, making it flesh in our lives, we will be transformed into the very image of the unseen God, taking on His nature and character, His omniscience, omnipotence, and omnipresence, His holiness, righteousness, and purity, His mercy, love, and compassion, as our inheritance from the Father of lights, with whom there is no variation, nor shadow of turning.

God's desire, as clearly portrayed in His Word, is to sovereignly speak and act through His chosen people, His children, His nation of kings and priests. Be not mistaken—this will come to pass. The only question is: Will you be part of what God is doing or not? The benefits to believing God's Word are more numerous than the sand of the sea. When we fully yield our lives to Him, we will experience what it truly means to be saved—saved from sin, death, hell, and the grave; saved from sickness and disease, and every effect of the curse. Our only responsibility is to believe that it is true!

So, let the Word become flesh in your life. Let the Spirit wield His mightiest weapon through you. Let the God of the universe manifest the magnitude of His power and the sovereignty of His will through you.

*And He said to them, "Go into all the world and **preach the gospel** to every creature. **He who believes and is baptized will be saved**; but he who does not believe will be condemned. And these **signs will follow those who believe**: In My name they will cast out demons; they will speak with new tongues; they will take up serpents; and if they drink anything deadly, it will by no means hurt them; they will lay hands on the sick, and they will recover (Mark 16:15-18).*

Timeless Truths From Chapter Four

- God only works with the God-seed He sows.

- God works with us to the degree that we harmonize with His will.

- I'm in the name and you're in the name—God is in the midst.

- Without the fulfillment of God's Word, His will can never be brought to fruition.

- God subjects Himself to Himself.

- The Word inside you has an assignment to a specific person or group that God has for you.

Endnotes

1. James Strong, *The New Strong's Expanded Exhaustive Concordance of the Bible: Strong's Expanded Dictionary of the Words in the Hebrew Bible* (Nashville, TN: Thomas Nelson Pub., 2001), 4.

2. Ibid.

CHAPTER FIVE

Toward a Working Relationship

THE DEPTHS OF GOD'S WORD

BASED on what we have learned in the last four chapters, we should now be moving toward a deep understanding of the working relationship between the Spirit of God and the Word of God within us. The greatest key to unlocking this relationship in our lives is the principle of continually feeding our spirits with the Word of God.

The Word of God is the often-neglected starting place for developing a meaningful relationship with our Heavenly Father. There is a prevailing mentality in the Body of Christ that maintains that Christian growth has little or nothing to do with how much of the Word we read on our own between Monday and Saturday. Yet how can people who neglect to partake of the manna of God's Word for six days of the week, also expect to sustain a "good relationship" with

God from the measly amount of Scripture that they receive on Sunday morning? It seems a very strange idea to me that a sermon once a week from the pastor, which is actually a product of his own relationship with God, is somehow supposed to be the creative basis for the whole congregation's relationship to God!

If I took this attitude in my marriage, then I would expect my natural dad to sit down with me once a week and tell me how to have a relationship with my wife based on his interactions with her in the last week! That is absolutely ridiculous. How can any relationship achieve a high level of intimacy from 30 minutes of interaction and fellowship per week? It just does not work that way. This kind of behavior eventually produces a large group of people who call themselves mature Christians and at the same time barely know God. We cannot approach our relationship with God as if we can take Him or leave Him at any time.

If we place a high value in God's Word, reverencing and respecting it, we can have an expectation to encounter God; for God and His Word are one.

It is our dependence on—or our negligence of—God's Word that really shows our hunger and thirst for God. If a person is truly hungry and thirsty for God and seeks for Him with all of his heart, his hunger and thirst will inevitably lead him to the Word of God.

We can always tell where a person's heart is at by what they spend their time doing. Whether we realize it or not, we always spend the most of our time doing what we love the best. If we love money above all else, then we will work more than anything else; if we love people above all else, then we will seek the love of others more than anything else. Time spent in God's Word, mining the depths of His Spirit for the mysteries of God's nature and character, demonstrates to God that we are serious about Him.

As believers we need to remember that whatever we meditate on will take dominion in our lives. If we want to develop a working relationship between the Word of God and the Spirit of God, we will need to meditate on the Word, giving the Holy Spirit something of Himself within us to attract Him. Remember what David said about the importance of God's Word in His own life:

I have rejoiced in the way of Your testimonies, as much as in all riches. I will meditate on Your precepts, and contemplate Your ways. I will delight myself in Your statutes; I will not forget Your Word (Psalm 119:14-16).

David was a man, who, according to the Scriptures, exemplified God's heart, and it is clear from the Psalms that David put great stock in the words of God. When his enemies would come against him, David would comfort himself with the Word. It is obvious that David's great intimacy with the Lord was centered on the Word.

Even Jesus was a lover of the written Word! He studied it and found His own identity as the Messiah in it. If this is true for Jesus Christ, the Living Word, how much more should we rely on the Word to feed our spirits and to draw near to God?

Be diligent to present yourself approved to God, a worker who does not need to be ashamed, rightly dividing the word of truth (2 Timothy 2:15).

Our success as children of God is tied directly to our response to the Word. Look carefully at the above verse. Paul is telling his spiritual son Timothy that if you desire to truly present yourself approved before God, then you must be able to rightly divide the Word of truth.

Remember, it is our response to the Word of truth, the Gospel of Jesus Christ, that saves us. In order to grow in knowledge and understanding of God we must be able to do more than just respond to another person's teaching of the Word. Every child of God must make it their priority to train their minds and mouths with the Word. The Scripture says that God's people perish for lack of knowledge. To remain foolish when there lies before you a vast ocean of wisdom will be destructive to your growth and progress in the Word. Ignorance will cost you more over time than any other sin; it will keep you poor, sick, and dissatisfied.

The prophet Isaiah describes some of the leaders of Judah, who were full of ignorance and laziness:

His watchmen are blind, they are all ignorant; they are all dumb dogs, they cannot bark; sleeping, lying down, loving to slumber. Yes, they are greedy dogs which never have enough. And they are shepherds who cannot understand; they all look to their own way, every one for his own gain, from his own territory (Isaiah 56:10-11).

These men were the blind leading the blind, as Jesus said. They pretended to know God, but in actuality, they were full of ignorance and laziness. Their lives were full of iniquity because they had forsaken the Word of God, and instead did things according to how they felt like doing them. This is what happens when we neglect the Word of God. It is meant to be our life and our sustenance; if we do not take in the strength and nourishment of the Word, we will surely die.

The solution to the epidemic of ignorance is a simple one: run hard after the Word. Develop a hunger for Him by drenching your spirit in His Word. Search in them to know the truth and to progress in the things of God. Proverbs 3:7-8, says, *"Do not be wise in your own eyes; fear the Lord and depart from evil. It will be health to your flesh, and strength to your bones,"* and Proverbs 1:7 says that the fear of the Lord is the beginning of knowledge.

You have to recognize that it goes beyond reading a book. When you stir up your passion for God's Word, you will actually be stirring up passion for the mind of God, the inner workings of His Spirit; you will be awakening your desire for the very heartbeat of God. The hungrier you are for God's Word, the more of it God will reveal to you. Jesus said, *"Blessed are those who hunger and thirst after righteousness, for they shall be filled."*

It is a God-working-with-God principle that as you fill your spirit with God's Word, you will have opportunities to sow it (what you sow, you will also reap)! Ultimately, God will pour into you an ever-increasing amount of revelatory knowledge that will set you, everyone around you, and the nations of the world, completely free.

It is the glory of God to conceal a matter, but the glory of kings is to search out a matter (Proverbs 25:2).

This verse reveals something interesting about God's sovereignty also. Do not be mistaken—it is not true that God wants to hide things from us, or gets some kind of pleasure from people's lack of understanding. Rather God will hide His glory and His revelation to stir up the hunger and passion of His children, until they seek for Him with all their might.

God is not interested in lukewarm love. He does not respond to anything but His own nature and character, and, as Hebrews 12:29 says, *"Our God is a consuming fire."* God will pull the veil over certain aspects of His essence until we get so hungry that we will do anything to have more of Him, until we are consumed with the desire to see God face to face.

In this way, God is producing soldiers whose faces are set like flint to know God; they will not be dissuaded, nor will they turn to the right hand or to the left. These people are willing to wrestle with God all night until He speaks His Word over them. They are not easily discouraged, because they have tasted and seen that the Lord is good, and they will not indulge long in the foolish entanglements of this world to be sidetracked from their purpose. They are neither foolish, nor are they lazy. They seek the Lord on their bed at night, and rise early to run to His courts. These people are not moved by what they see; rather the Word—the supernatural, all-powerful voice of the sovereign God of the universe—moves them.

By hiding His face for a short season, God turns fair-weather friends into passionate lovers of God. By creating one spark, God has set the whole fire ablaze, and in the end, will burn down the whole forest, changing a whole ecosystem. That is the reason why it brings so much glory to God to conceal a matter; what God has concealed will be sought by His kings.

We have to realize the power locked in one revelation from the Word of God. Do you know that one living Word can give you breakthrough in every area of your life? It can cause you to climb a thousand mountains and go places that you never thought possible. For example, I am sure that many who read this book have read the verse in Isaiah 40, which says:

But those who wait on the Lord shall renew their strength; they shall mount up with wings like eagles, they shall run and not be weary, they shall walk and not faint (Isaiah 40:31).

When I minister this message I bring a tallit to give a visual demonstration of what the word "wait" in Hebrew means. A tallit is a Hebrew prayer shawl that Jesus would have worn every day. The exact Hebrew word for "wait" is *qavah*, defined as "to twist, to bind like a rope, to be strong and robust from the idea of binding fast." When you look at the strands of rope you see three strands twisted together to make one strong cord. The longest strand used to wrap the other strands is known as the Shamesh. Truly the Holy Spirit is the only one who can wrap our lives and the life of the Lord together. The picture painted here is: As we intertwine with God, we will be made strong.

Can you picture yourself soaring above the clouds like an eagle? If it is hard to picture yourself flying, what about the second part of the verse? "*They shall run and not grow weary.*" Can you picture yourself running a 26K and not even losing breath? Well, what if you could? What would it do to change your perspective in tough circumstances? I know that, if I am flying like an eagle, I am soaring above the clouds and storms of life. The trials of the natural world cannot touch me where I am. I am flying high, looking into the sun, and I am completely free.

This one verse could take care of any anxiety I might be dealing with, fear or worry issues, which as we all know, can cause a lot of ailments in the body. Ulcers of the stomach, constipation, high blood pressure, blood sugar problems, rashes, and many other sicknesses are caused by anxiety. Do you see that having a revelation of this one verse can set you free from all of that? The Word gives us God's perspective on the circumstances in our lives that seem so difficult. In God's covenant eyes, however, the victory is already ours.

COVENANT RELATIONSHIP

In the previous chapter, I touched briefly on covenant, and what it means to be in covenant with God. There are different aspects of covenant because there are actually different kinds of covenant. All of them, however, demonstrate a binding and eternal pact that cannot be disbanded, except under certain circumstances.

There is one aspect in which all covenants are alike; that is, covenant is always sealed through blood. For example, among pagan nations, the two parties would cut their forearms or their hands and then press them together or shake hands. The mixing of their blood signified that the two people had become one, of one mind and one heart. They would also eat a meal together, each partaking of the same bread and meat. The eating of the meal signified that as the bread and meat were now part of their bodies, so the covenant and the very lives of the other group of people was now part of them. This sort of covenant took place between smaller nations and tribes of people so that when a larger power came against one of the covenantal tribes, those who had become their allies would have to fight with them against the greater power.

This type of covenant signifies a certain level of intimacy, in that the two parties now acted as if they were not separate, but one group. They had free trade alliances, so that they could help each other without the cost of taxes and duties. As you know, these sorts of covenants still exist today between nations of the free world and can be a very controversial subject within the realm of politics.

So, we see that when God cut covenant with Abraham, the Lord had Abraham prepare two bulls cut in two. The Lord then put Abraham in a deep sleep and walked between the halves of the two bulls, signifying that God was cutting an everlasting covenant with Abraham. This covenant was sealed with the blood of the slaughtered animals. Symbolically then, we see that all of the male children in Abraham's family were circumcised on the eighth day, symboliz-ing the blood covenant between the children of Israel and the Lord God.

Another type of covenant is very well-known to all of us; its importance and eternality, however, has been downplayed and tar-nished by the liberalism and relativism in modern society. The covenant of which I speak is marriage. This covenant, as we all know, is also sealed with blood; it is the blood that is spilt during intimacy, a very private ceremony between a husband and his wife. Under the old covenant law, the actual act of celebrating blood covenant between a man and a woman (in other words, sexual intercourse) meant that they had become married. Intimacy was not separate from marriage, nor was marriage separate from intimacy. In fact, any one caught devaluing or misusing the act of celebrating blood covenant was taken outside the city gates and stoned.

Moses did allow for divorce, or the destruction of blood covenant between a man and a woman, under certain cases. However, Jesus teaches us that, in God's eyes, the marriage covenant is eternal because the two have become one.

It is important to note here how the Law of Reciprocity operates within covenant. When we are walking in intimacy with God, we are truly married to Him; we have become one with Him. We all know that a love relationship is a two-sided deal. As Jesus says in Luke, "*Give and it shall be given unto you.*" Releasing love to God creates a doorway for God to release more and more of His love in our own lives. God is love. God loves those who love Him. First John 4:7-8 (NASB) says, "*Beloved, let us love one another, for love is from God; and everyone who loves is born of God and knows God. The one who does not love does not know God, for God is love.*" First Corinthians 8:3 (NASB) says, "*but if anyone loves God, he is known by Him.*"

Worship is a powerful force that opens up a channel between God's throne and our hearts to receive God's power, His nature and character. Loving God through worship is a very important part of abiding in Him. When we walk in love, we will keep His commandments. In so doing God said He would take sickness and disease far away from us. And as Psalm 91 says, if you abide in (love) the secret place, or the place of intimacy, no evil can befall you.

*Anytime you walk out the nature of God,
you silence spiritual warfare.*

But just as it is written, "Things which eye has not seen and ear has not heard, and which have not entered the heart of man, all that God has prepared for those who love [God] Him" (1 Corinthians 2:9 NASB).

The point to this discourse is to demonstrate to you the binding qualities of covenant, and its importance in the sight of the Father. Covenant is the place of intimacy, a place where the bride and the bridegroom become one, where we become united with Christ. The word covenant connotes two people walking together, side by side, always present to help at a moment's notice. The word actually means to bind together! Covenant is more than casual friendship and goes beyond neighborly duties. Covenant says that the two parties involved will lay down their lives for the other party. Covenant is serious business!

THE BREAD OF COVENANT WALKING IN THE MIDST

Now behold, two of them were traveling that same day to a village called Emmaus, which was seven miles from Jerusalem. And they talked together of all these things which had happened. So it was, while they conversed and reasoned, that Jesus Himself drew near and went with them. But their eyes were restrained, so that they did not know Him. ...And beginning at Moses and all the Prophets, He expounded to them in all the Scriptures the things concerning Himself. Then they drew near to the village where they were going, and He indicated that He would have gone farther. But they constrained Him, saying, "Abide with us, for it is toward evening, and the day is far spent." And He went in to stay with them. Now it came to pass, as He sat at the table with them, that He took bread, blessed and broke it, and gave it to them. Then their eyes were opened and they knew Him; and He vanished from their sight. And they said to one another, "Did not our heart burn within us while He talked with us on the road, and while He opened the Scriptures to us?" (Luke 24:13-16, 27-32).

There is so much I could connect here of the God-working-with-God principle. Let's begin with: God is attracted to God. Here these two men are speaking about the Christ and He appears to them. How? God was attracted to God. God-words were coming out of their mouths.

The man who had done the impossible, healing the sick and raising the dead, casting out demons and cleansing the lepers, the man whom God had raised from the dead was walking down the road with them! I ask you, how is that possible? We have this same struggle in the Body of Christ today. Yes, we have the miracle-working Savior walking in our midst even as we speak. Our eyes are not on the face of the One who calmed the water and raised the dead, however. Our eyes are too consumed with looking at our own circumstances to see that the answer is right in front of us.

So what did Jesus do? What He had always done and will always do: sow Himself so that He has something to work with (verse 27). In sowing Himself, He unveiled the prophetic Scriptures concerning the Messiah. That is why in verse 28 when He acted as if He was going elsewhere that they invited Him to come stay with them. This is powerful. Once the intimacy of God working with God is established, then revelation can be unveiled. They received the Word that had become flesh by inviting Him to stay, just as Mary had (*"Be it unto me…"*).

As the men listened to Jesus describe how it was prophesied of Him that He must suffer and die, and be raised to life again, their hearts burned within them. It is as if the Spirit was stirring the hearts of these men, and yet they still could not grasp who was in their midst. They did not realize that the Fulfillment of the Law was standing next to them. The One who was anointed to remove their burdens and destroy their yokes was among them. When they neared the place where they were staying they knew that they must compel Jesus to stay with them, yet they did not know why. The principle of God working with God was in motion by attraction. God was attracted to God. It was only after Jesus had broken the bread and handed it to them that their eyes were opened to the reality of the Christ.

For with You is the fountain of life; in Your light we see light (Psalm 36:9).

I pray that the eyes of your heart may be enlightened, so that you will know… (Ephesians 1:18 NASB).

The revelation of covenant will open our eyes to the Living Word who is truly in our midst. We are actually in covenant with a resurrected, immortal Man, who now sits on the throne of God, ever making intercession for us. The One who overcame death, hell, sin, and the grave, has become one with us through blood covenant— His own blood, which was spilt on the Cross to close the barrier between God and us. God the Father cut covenant with God the Word on the Cross, so that we could step into the supernatural overflow of that divine relationship.

All the blessings and abundance of God are mine through covenant. All of God's riches, His life, His fullness, His power, grace, love, knowledge, wisdom, and justice are my inheritance through Christ Jesus our Lord. Do you see that was actually the Living Word that became the perfect Sacrifice on our behalf? It was the Word that cut covenant with God through His own blood, thereby ending the enmity between God and man! Through the Living Word, we now have access to all the blessings of the written Word, the covenant that God has spoken for Himself and for us. We should have total confidence in the Word of God, that all of His promises are Yes and Amen!

This again reveals the importance of God's Word in our lives. It is the bread of the covenant. When we nourish our bodies with bread, it literally becomes part of our beings. The Scripture says in John 6:51, "*I am the living bread that came down out of heaven; if anyone eats of this bread, he will live forever; and the bread also which I will give for the life of the world is My flesh.*" In the same way God wants to permeate our beings with His Word, creating a doorway for Him to infuse you and infiltrate you with His grace and truth.

Keep in mind what John chapter 1 says: "*The Word became flesh and dwelt among us; and we have beheld His glory, the glory of the only begotten of the Father, full of grace and truth.*" When the Word of the covenant, the Bread of life, becomes one with us, spirit, soul, and body, His Word will become flesh in us, and we will behold His glory full of grace and truth.

God wants to brand you with His Word in the same manner that He cut away the foreskins of the Israelite men. He wants the foreskin of our hearts to be cut away so that we can be saturated with the power of His Word. He wants to cut away the outer layers of unbelief, religion, fear, and ignorance, until He reaches the soft and tender flesh of our hearts, still impressionable and teachable, able to be restored to the image of the Word.

APPLYING THE WORD

Though it was many years ago, I remember clearly the day I received an amazing revelation concerning Isaiah 10:27. I was driving down the road in the middle of nowhere, when suddenly I got a headache. Immediately this Scripture came to me and I began to repeat this verse over and over again.

> *It shall come to pass in that day that his burden will be taken away from your shoulder, and his yoke from your neck, and the yoke will be destroyed because of the anointing oil* (Isaiah 10:27).

I said, "Lord, You said the anointing removes burdens and destroys yokes. I declare this headache will be removed and this yoke will be destroyed." As I gave voice to God (the Word) inside me, God was becoming a part of me, just as the bread I eat becomes a part of my flesh. When the revelation of that verse finally exploded in me, I started shouting, "I got it!" I received a revelation of my covenant relationship with God and the rights and privileges that go along with it. The Scripture says it shall come to pass on that day. My spirit said, today is that day! The Scripture says that his burden shall be taken off my shoulder and his yoke from off my neck, and the yoke will be destroyed because of the anointing. My spirit said, every burden has been removed and every yoke has been destroyed because Christ is in you, the hope of glory. My spirit received a great big "YES!" from God, as the revelation of the Word of His covenant became flesh in my body. The revelation of that one Scripture became so powerful in me that immediately the headache left me and I was totally free from pain.

When truth takes on wings,
you will discover total freedom.

It is important to continually meditate on the Word. It contains all of the promises that God has given us through His covenant. We have to allow the seed of the Word to germinate in our hearts until it has taken root and sprouted. Soon it will grow and become a huge tree, ready to produce much fruit. In order for our hearts to become rooted and grounded in the Word, we have to fill our minds with it both night and day. We have to meditate on the things of God instead of the things of men, washing our minds and hearts with the water of the Word, and allowing the blood of the covenant to cleanse our conscience from every dead work to serve the living God. Once the revelation of the Word has taken hold of you, no one will be able to take it from you. It becomes a shield against the lies of the enemy and a weapon in the hand of the Spirit of God to destroy the strongholds of tradition, empty ideas, and philosophies of men.

COVENANT RELATIONSHIP THROUGH PARABLES

There is an interesting aspect of covenant relationship that we see demonstrated in Jesus' use of parables in His teaching. Parables are a method through which God's Spirit can convey the mysteries of God to our spirit. The word *parable* comes from the Greek word "*parabole* (par-ab-ol-ay); a similitude ("parable"), i.e., symbolically, fictitious narrative (of common life conveying a moral), apothegm or adage; in the King James Version, it may be translated as comparison, figure, parable, or proverb." The synoptic Gospels are full of excellent examples of apothegms and adages—stories that are figurative and represent hidden or concealed truths, which are indirectly communicated. It is important to know why Jesus chose to teach in parables.

Matthew 13:9-12 explains to us why Jesus used this method of communication when teaching the masses.

> *"He who has ears to hear, let him hear!" And the disciples came and said to Him, "Why do You speak to them in parables?" He answered and said to them, "Because it has been given to you to know the mysteries of the kingdom of heaven, but to them it has not been given. For whoever has, to him more will be given, and he will have abundance; but whoever does not have, even what he has will be taken away from him"* (Matthew 13:9-12).

At the beginning of this passage, Jesus has just ended the parable of the sower and the seed. He has been teaching a great multitude of people who were not His disciples. These people are drawn to Him, not for the sake of the Word, as Jesus proclaims later, but because of the bread that He had given them and the miracles He had performed. The people are not interested in being trained; rather, they want their bellies full and their needs met.

Of course Jesus does not turn them away or refuse to teach them. Instead, He veils His words by using parables, exposing the motive of the heart. Honestly, the Jews of that day as a whole were not overly educated people. We have to remember that, after the return from the Babylonian captivity, the children of Israel were never again a free nation. After the Babylonians, it was the Greeks, and after the Greeks, it was the Roman Empire. The Jews were a nation in captivity. The only version of the truth these men and women knew came from the mouths of the Sadducees and Pharisees; Jesus presented to them a God of love and freedom.

The truth is that Jesus chose not to reveal the deep secrets of His Kingdom to anyone except those who were in close relationship with Him—His disciples. Relationship is what opened the door for the disciples to receive the deeper revelations of the Kingdom of God. Interestingly enough, the disciples also did not understand the parable the first time they heard one. If these men who walked and talked with Jesus could not understand the words of Jesus, how then would the multitude understand, who had not spent any one-on-one time with the Lord?

Parables are mysteries intended for revelation through relationship and discipleship.

When Jesus cried out to the multitude, "*He who has ears to hear, let him hear,*" the Lord was trying to open the hearts of the people to their own ignorance. He was saying to them, "Do you understand what I am saying? If not, then you do not have your spiritual ears turned on, nor can you receive the things of the Kingdom. If the simplest story is complicated to you, how then will you receive the greater matters of the Spirit?" This is the same response that Jesus gave to His disciples when they asked for the meaning of the parable in Mark 4:13. Jesus was trying to convey truth from His Spirit to theirs. He wanted to bypass their mind and emotion and to reach the spirit within them to hear and receive the truth.

I have also seen this with the people whom God has given me to mentor. Sometimes, manifestations of the flesh, such as fear, rejection, or rebellion, will stand between a person and the truth. In order to bypass what might be their natural response to correction, I will tell them a story containing the truth I want them to apply to their lives. In this way, I have ministered the Word of God from the Spirit of God within me to their spirit. On one occasion Jesus did this with the Pharisees.

> Then He began to speak to them in parables: "A man planted a vineyard and set a hedge around it, dug a place for the wine vat and built a tower. And he leased it to vinedressers and went into a far country. Now at vintage-time he sent a servant to the vinedressers, that he might receive some of the fruit of the vineyard from the vinedressers. And they took him and beat him and sent him away empty-handed. ... Therefore still having one son, his beloved, he also sent him to them last, saying, 'They will respect my son.' But those vinedressers said among themselves, 'This is the heir. Come, let us kill him, and the inheritance will be ours.' So they took him and killed him and cast him out of the vineyard. Therefore what will the owner of the vineyard do? He will come and destroy the vinedressers, and give the vineyard to others." ...And they sought to lay hands on Him, but feared the multitude, for they knew He had spoken the parable against them. So they left Him and went away (Mark 12:1-3, 6-9,12).

Do you see that these Pharisees had their spiritual ears open to hear the message that Jesus was trying to convey to their spirits? They heard the truth and were cut to the quick; you could even say they were convicted! Yet they hardened their hearts to the truth, and then consulted among themselves to fulfill the prophetic words of the parable. They had no relationship, no covenant with the Messiah that would create a working relationship between His Spirit and theirs, so that their hearts would be open to receive the correction of God's Son.

All of this talk about parables reminds me of another parable. The incident of which I speak is when David had taken Bathsheba, gotten her pregnant, and then had her husband killed to cover the whole thing up. What a mess this man after God's own heart had put himself in! Soon there was a knock on David's door, however.

Then the Lord sent Nathan to David. And he came to him, and said to him: "There were two men in one city, one rich and the other poor. The rich man had exceedingly many flocks and herds. But the poor man had nothing, except one little ewe lamb which he had bought and nourished; and it grew up together with him and with his children. It ate of his own food and drank from his own cup and lay in his bosom; and it was like a daughter to him. And a traveler came to the rich man, who refused to take from his own flock and from his own herd to prepare one for the wayfaring man who had come to him; but he took the poor man's lamb and prepared it for the man who had come to him." So David's anger was greatly aroused against the man, and he said to Nathan, "As the Lord lives, the man who has done this shall surely die! And he shall restore fourfold for the lamb, because he did this thing and because he had no pity." Then Nathan said to David, "You are the man! Thus says the Lord God of Israel: 'I anointed you king over Israel, and I delivered you from the hand of Saul. I gave you your master's house and your master's wives into your keeping, and gave you the house of Israel and Judah. And if that had been too little, I also would have given you much more! Why have you despised the commandment of the Lord, to do evil in His sight? You have killed Uriah the Hittite with the sword; you have taken his wife to be your wife, and have killed him with the sword of the people of Ammon. Now therefore, the sword shall never depart from your house, because you have despised Me, and have taken the wife of Uriah the Hittite to be your wife.' ... So David said to Nathan, "I have sinned against the Lord." And Nathan said to David, "The Lord also has put away your sin; you shall not die. However, because by this deed you have given great occasion to the enemies of the Lord to blaspheme, the child also who is born to you shall surely die" (2 Samuel 12:1-10, 13-14).

Because David was in covenant relationship with the Lord, there was a working relationship between the Spirit of God and David's spirit. David also had great respect for the prophet of God, Nathan, and therefore David's heart was open to Nathan to receive correction from him. The man of God spoke a parable so that David would see for himself that the sins he had committed were terribly displeasing to God. Once David's spirit heard and received the truth of the parable, Nathan could bring the correction of God in the king's life. Now let's go back to the parable in Matthew 13.

Therefore I speak to them in parables, because seeing they do not see, and hearing they do not hear, nor do they understand. And in them the prophecy of Isaiah is fulfilled, which says: "Hearing you will hear and shall not understand, and seeing you will see and not perceive; for the hearts of this people have grown dull. Their ears are hard of hearing, and their eyes they have closed, lest they should see with their eyes and hear with their ears, lest they should understand with their hearts and turn, so that I should heal them" (Matthew 13:13-15).

The less a person feeds their spirit with the Word of God, the less the Holy Spirit will have to work with to produce God in our lives. The issue is not my ability to hear in the natural. In fact, my ears work very well. The problem we all face is that it takes more than the natural hearing of the Word for it to come to pass in our lives. It takes knowing it in your knower, as Oral Roberts says. It takes receiving the Word in your spirit. God is a spirit; therefore, His Spirit wants to communicate directly with your spirit, as He works with the Word that has been planted in your heart. God has a desire to build a spirit-to-spirit connection between you and Himself, and also between the members of the Body of Christ.

When we are communicating with each other through the spirit instead of through our flesh and emotions, God will be able to minister His Word through us to others with much more clarity and precision. The revelation of spirit-to-spirit relationships will be discussed in greater detail in the upcoming book, *GWWG: Spirit to Spirit*.

TRUTH HAS EARS

In order for the truth of God to set us free, we must first receive the Truth in our hearts. We have to be intimately acquainted with the Truth before truth can set truth free. If we are deceived in our hearts, and are living in subjection to the father of lies, we have denied the truth and therefore cannot be set free by it.

As He spoke these words, many believed in Him. Then Jesus said to those Jews who believed Him, "If you abide in My word,

*you are My disciples indeed. And you shall know the truth, and
the truth shall make you free"* (John 8:30-32).

---

*First you must know the truth; then the One (Jesus),
who is the Truth, the Way, and the Life,
will set truth free.*

We will not be set free just by hearing the truth with our natural ears. If we acknowledge that the Word is God, and if we see that
the Word is also the Way, the Truth, and the Life, we will have
believed in our hearts and become obedient to it in our spirit, soul,
and body. Remember, John chapter 1 says that the Word of God is
full of grace and truth! Truth has the ability to hear the Word of God
and obey it. Unrenewed, unsubmitted flesh does not have this ability. Keep in mind: Truth is going across the airways all the time, so in
itself it does not have the ability to set anyone free. First you must
receive and become intimately acquainted with the truth and then
truth can set you free.

---

*Truth only sets truth free in the same way
God only sets God free.*

Do you remember what Paul said to the Corinthians? It is the Spirit of God that searches the deep things of God, and only the mind of Christ, the mind that is anointed and washed clean in the water of the Word, can receive the things that the Spirit is revealing about the Father. Truth has ears. Truth sets truth free! Once truth has gotten on the inside of you, it will create a channel for the Spirit of God to go to work with the Truth. It is truth in our hearts that will unlock the mysteries hidden within parables, because it has the power to recognize its own kind.

Truth is full of discernment; it can see a lie coming for miles. It is the truth of God's Word in our hearts that will produce a check in us when a person's emotions speak louder than the Spirit of God within them. However, when the Spirit of God is speaking clearly through a person, the Truth in us will go to work with the Truth in them to unlock the mysteries of God.

⁂

When a person's soul or flesh speaks louder than their spirit, you will have a check; but when their spirit speaks louder than their soul or flesh, you will have peace.

⁂

The Scripture teaches us that the Word produces belief in its hearers. The Word must have a place in you. If the Word of God has no place in you, then you will not be able to hear God.

I know that you are Abraham's descendants, but you seek to kill Me, because My word has no place in you. ...He who is of God hears God's words; therefore you do not hear, because you are not of God (John 8:37,47).

The Word of God opens your spiritual ears to hear God; because God only hears what is of God. That is why Isaiah 43:26 says that God wants us to put Him in remembrance of His covenant.

And when he brings out his own sheep, he goes before them; and the sheep follow him, for they know his voice. ...My sheep hear My voice, and I know them, and they follow Me (John 10:4,27).

*Pilate therefore said to Him, "Are You a king then?" Jesus answered, "You say rightly that I am a king. For this cause I was born, and for this cause I have come into the world, that I should bear witness to the truth. Everyone who is of the **truth hears My voice**"* (John 18:37).

TRUTH HAS EARS!

There are several distinctive Hebrew words that can be translated "to hear" in English. The two most commonly used in the Old Testament are the words anah and shama. Anah means "to eye, to head, to pay attention to, and, by implication, to respond." This word connotes action also. In Isaiah 48:8, God says, "*In an acceptable time I have heard [anah] you, and in a day of salvation I have helped you,*" paralleling hearing with helping. In this specific verse, hearing and helping are one and the same.

Shama also means to hear; this time with the implication of obedience. The word is actually translated "to obey" and also in the adjective form, "obedient." Shama also means to understand and discern intelligently. In other words, if I tell my young son to take out the trash and he does not obey me, in God's eyes that means he never heard me in the first place. According to the Scripture, to hear is to obey. John testifies of this same truth in his Gospel.

We have to recognize what will create a clear channel into a person's heart so that the Truth of the Word can be sown in their lives. Some people have been hurt in the past because the messenger sent to speak the truth did not speak it in love. If I come to them and try to preach hell fire and brimstone to them, they won't be able to receive it because of past offense. There are some cases where releasing the influence of God's love is the most powerful force to open them up to the truth. People are desperate for love. If we create a clear path into their hearts through the continual grace of God's love, it will soften the hardened ground of their hearts to receive the engrafted Word of God, which is able to save their souls.

GRACE: GOD'S INFLUENCE UPON THE HEART

Have you ever had a close friend or relative who always wanted to spend time with you? This person would call you every day, just to see how you were doing; he or she would come by your place of work and bring you gifts. This person knew your schedule and respected your time. This person valued your wisdom and asked you for prayer. He or she could tell what you needed without you even speaking, and also knew how to solve the problem. This person was reliable and faithful—a servant, through and through. Have you ever known someone like this? They are a pearl of great price, and yet they are full of humility and love and do not exalt themselves because of their service!

Do you know that God wants people like this in His life? The Scripture says that He is going to and fro over the face of the earth looking for a heart that is loyal to Him! He is interested in people who are interested in Him, no matter what it costs them. Some people may say that we should not harass God or push issues with God; I promise you, however, if you get in God's face, God will get in yours. Draw near to God and He will draw near to you.

This principle applies when we are seeking truth in God's Word. Even though we might not recognize it when we first start searching for it, once we start discovering what the truth is, we will also realize Who the Truth is! Jesus said, "*I am the Way, the Truth, and the Life.*" The more we seek the truth in God's Word, the more our eyes will be opened to see that we are actually seeking Jesus, and He is always faithful to reveal Himself to people who seek Him. "*Seek and you shall find,*" Jesus said. Remember the Lord never said anything flippantly; He never said anything He did not mean with His whole heart. God does not change His mind. What God says is the final Word on every subject.

There is actually a litmus test for whether or not something is truth. For example, if we are sitting in a church service and we hear something that we have never heard before, we must ask ourselves the question: Does it reveal God's essence? Truth will always reveal God. The second question we have to ask ourselves is: Is the statement being made coupled with love? Ephesians 4 teaches us that if the truth is going to equip the Body of Christ to grow, it must be spoken in love. Remember Jesus is the living Word—He is the perfect testimony of the living God; in Christ dwells the fullness of the Godhead bodily, and all of who God is was fully revealed through Him. Our definition of truth must be based on Jesus Christ, who is the Truth.

Truth is utterly important when we study what God's grace is and how it is intricately part of who we are in Christ. Remember what John said: The glory that is revealed through the Word of God became flesh is full of grace and truth. It is actually the Spirit of God working with the Word of God, the truth, in our lives that will produce an abundance of grace toward us.

The Greek word, which is translated as "grace," is *charis*. This word essentially means "the divine influence upon the heart and its reflection in the life." It is the truth of God's Word that influences us with God's divine nature and character. His Spirit works with the Word of God to create a reflection of God's holiness, perfection, righteousness, love, mercy, and goodness. God wants to engrave His Word on our hearts so that our lives will reflect His divinity. God's Word is the avenue through which grace, or the divine influence on the heart and its reflection in the life, is transferred to us.

I heard another minister say this, "Revelation says, 'I see'; recognition says 'I see God'; relationship declares 'I see God with me'; reflection shouts 'I see God in me!'" What counts is what our hearts are reflecting. See the fullness of the nature of God working in you! Because the Word is God, our receptiveness to it determines the level of grace that we are going to walk in. Do you remember what the writer of Hebrews has to say about the Word?

> *For the word of God is living and powerful, and sharper than any two-edged sword, piercing even to the division of soul and spirit, and of joints and marrow, and is a discerner of the thoughts and intents of the heart. And there is no creature hidden from His sight, but all things are naked and open to the eyes of Him to whom we must give account* (Hebrews 4:12-13).

The Word is like a huge floodlight in a prison yard. If there is anything running around in the dark that should not be there, that huge light is going to expose it really quickly! If there are things in our heart that have not been dealt with, things we have attempted to hide from God and from the godly people in our lives, the Word will cut to the center of our beings, exposing any darkness trying to run from the transforming power of God's Word. Once that darkness has been exposed, the washing of the water of the Word can eliminate it. This creates an individual who can correctly and transparently reflect God's grace and truth. When God looks at us He should see a reflection of His glory, His awesome power, character, and abilities. Remember that God is not weak toward us in any way, nor will He show Himself weak through us if we will simply yield to His Word.

It may be that the thought has crossed your mind about the cost of being totally transparent and open before God, allowing Him to root out and destroy every bit of darkness in our lives that is hindering us from fully reflecting the glorious image of the Son, Jesus Christ. Remember the price that Christ had to pay for you! God is a totally transparent spirit; there is no spot or darkness in Him. He is the epicenter of all light, radiating from the innermost part of His being. To be transparent is to be like God!

God's desire is to be completely exposed and open with His bride, the Church; the only way He can do that is if the Church is perfectly reflecting God to Himself. God only comes into intimate relationship with Himself, because it is only God in intimate contact with God that will produce God. When God unveils Himself to us, it means that the Spirit of God and the Word of God have produced godliness in our lives. As God responds to Himself in us by giving us more revelation of who He is, our knowledge of God will grow, thus enlarging our capacity to receive God's grace—His divine influence! God working with God is a wonderful cycle of intimacy and productivity, which, once it begins, can never stop.

∽∽∞∽∽

It is only God in intimate contact with God that will produce what is of God.

∽∽∞∽∽

But we all, with unveiled face, beholding as in a mirror the glory of the Lord, are being transformed into the same image from glory to glory, just as by the Spirit of the Lord (2 Corinthians 3:18).

Paul is comparing our experience with God to the mountaintop experience that Moses had with God in the Book of Exodus. Paul makes the amazing claim that what we should be seeing and hearing from God every day is far greater and not to be compared with the glory that Moses experienced on the mountain. Paul states that the glory that shown in the face of Moses was fading away. In other words, it produced no lasting change; it did not take Moses from glory to glory, nor did it transform him into the image of the living God. In order for this to take place, Moses would have had to gaze intently on the face of God. Unfortunately this was not possible for Moses, for God had said, anyone who looks upon my face will die.

We know, however, that whoever gazes intently on the face of Jesus Christ will die—die to the flesh and its desires—and will take on the very life and substance of Jesus Christ Himself. Paul testifies to us in another place that whoever is in Christ is a new creature; the old man is dead and past away, and all things have become new. Once we have died, and our new life is hidden with Christ in God, the barrier between the face of God and us has been destroyed by the blood. We can now gaze intently on God's face, beholding His glory as if we were staring into a mirror and seeing His image us, and be transformed into that image which ever increases in glory and majesty by the Spirit of the Lord God. It is the Word through the blood who has broken down the walls of separation between God and us, and it is His Spirit that transforms us into His perfect likeness. These two make a powerful team to reconcile us fully to the Father.

GOD WORKING WITH GOD: SALVATION

Here is a guaranteed strategy for building yourself up on your most holy faith, stirring your passion for the Father; this will help you to remember who Christ is in you. Almost every person I know gets up in the morning and looks in the mirror. When I get up in the morning and look in the mirror, I am not always impressed by what I see. Instead of dwelling on what I do not like about myself, as many people do when they see their image in a mirror, I begin to speak what the Word of God says about me. For example, I will look myself in the eye and say: "Warren, you are an image bearer of God; and as He is, so are you in this world! You are daily overcoming the devil by the blood of the Lamb and the Word of your testimony. You are anointed by God to preach the Gospel to the nations. You are full of the Holy Spirit. You are overflowing with the power of God. You are a son of the I AM. Out of your belly flows a river of living water, and everywhere the river flows healing flows. You lay hands on the sick and they recover. You raise the dead and cast out demons, and no weapon formed against you will prosper!" Immediately, I will hear the voice of the Holy Spirit say, "That is right!"

I recognize what God has placed inside me, and this truth causes me to experience an awesome sense of intimacy, confirmation, confidence, and total security in God. I am not the one who is doing the work; it is the Spirit of God working with the Word of God that produces God's best in my life. God is the one who called you, drew you, and wooed you with His love; it is His grace that saved you.

No man can come to Me unless the Father who sent Me draws him; and I will raise him up at the last day (John 6:44).

Do you realize that salvation is a product of God working with God? In order for a person to be "saved," there has to be a God-working-with-God relationship established between God and His

Word. For example, I have heard many testimonies in which a person was continually bombarded by annoyingly happy people who just happened to run into him and tell him, by the way, Jesus loves you! This person did not even know who this Jesus character was, but because those few people kept going out of their way to tell him about His love, the unbeliever finally asked one of them, "Well, if this Jesus loves me, why doesn't He help me out once and a while?"

Now it is time for a sower to sow an anointed Word. Once the Word has been sown into a person's heart, the Spirit of God will begin to work with that Word, causing the convicting power of God to grow in that person's heart. God knows exactly what it will take to draw every person into His hand. God always does what it takes to chase you down with His influence. Once an unbeliever has heard the Word of God, he will either choose to accept it or reject it, although he may not have immediate conversion. That Word may have to cut through fear, doubt, unbelief, bitterness, confusion, and a hundred other distractions that the devil uses to cloud their minds with in order to hinder them from truly believing the Word and repenting.

However, once the Word is accepted, the Holy Spirit can produce what is needed for salvation. The unbeliever may come back to the Christian and say, "I want to hear more about Jesus." Of course this is an opportunity to plant more of God in his heart. The more of the Word that person gets inside of him, the more of God that the Spirit can produce. Soon, true belief has been produced in his heart and according to Romans 10:8-9 once the Word is near you even in your mouth and in your heart and you confess, then you are saved. When we confess that the Word became flesh, died, and conquered death, hell, the grave, and rose again, God hears Himself and when God hears His Word coming out of your mouth—God works with God and you are saved. One Word from the Holy Spirit can produce immediate God results.

This is demonstrated in Acts 10 with the conversion of Cornelius' household. They heard the Word, they received it in their hearts, the Spirit went to work with the Word, and they believed it in their hearts, calling Jesus their Lord in their inner man. At this point the Lord came to possess what was His, and a new creature was born and they spoke a new creature language. Jesus told His disciples in John 15:16:

> *You did not choose Me, but I chose you and appointed you that you should go and bear fruit, and that your fruit should remain, that whatever you ask the Father in My name He may give you.*

God is the one who determines the timing in which He will release His influence into your life. The process of God producing Himself in your life is a cycle, which God has preordained; it is a spiritual movement that takes us from glory to glory in the nature and character of God. As Ephesians 1:11 says, "*In Him* [God] *we have obtained an inheritance, being predestined according to the purpose of Him* [God] *who works all things according to the counsel of His* [God's] *will.*" He knows exactly what must happen in each person's life to produce enough of the reflection of Himself to take every believer to the next level in God.

God is the source of the God-potential inside of you! The idea is that as He places His potential inside of us, we will yield to it, making ourselves more and more available to the plan and vision of God, and thus giving God more and more of His own essence to work with. The more of God that is reflected in a person's life, the more is required of Him. Each level of growth and glory also includes an expectation on the part of God for us to manifest more holiness and purity. Once again we can see to whom much is given much is required. God will answer the hunger of God.

When we truly get hungry, we will learn that God is only released in our lives to the extent that we yield to the principles, which manifest the Kingdom of God. This is part of God's sovereignty that is misunderstood. He set in place principles, which, if applied, will immediately produce results. In order for our hunger for God, not only to be satisfied, but also to be expanded, we must make a deposit of the divine influence that we find in God's Word; His timing is based on what He has spoken. As we take in the Word, it will sustain us and flood our eyes with light to see the plan of God, including His sovereign timing as to when to release more of His potential in and through our spirits.

Draw near to God;
He will draw near to you.

The potential relationship that can be cultivated between our Spirit and God through His Word is a thing of surpassing beauty. It can be compared to a tender courtship. We are continually reading God's love letters to us, which stir up our desire for His personal presence, not just His beautiful words. The more we read of His devotion and desire for us, the more we hunger to be with Him, where He is. He is drawing us and wooing us with His Word, and as He draws us to His side, He is also continually drawing nearer to us through His Spirit. As we value His Word, God slowly opens our eyes to see Him, until the barriers that keep us from the face of God have been broken and we see Him as He is. John the beloved tells us in First John 3:2:

Beloved, now we are children of God; and it has not yet been revealed what we shall be, but we know that when He is revealed, we shall be like Him, for we shall see Him as He is.

As I read this verse I feel John's desperate desire for God. He is not satisfied with what he knows of God, but has a fervent expectation that drives him forward. John makes it clear to us that as we seek the Father, He will reveal Himself to us; As He shows Himself to us, unveiling to us His nature and character, we shall become like Him, because we will truly see God face to face. As we become one with God we will be consumed with what He is and will be swallowed up in His hugeness.

But when He, the Spirit of Truth (the Truth-giving Spirit) comes, He will guide you into all the Truth (the whole, full Truth). For He will not speak His own message [on His own authority]; but He will tell whatever He hears [from the Father; He will give the message that has been given to Him], and He will announce and declare to you the things that are to come [that will happen in the future] (John 16:13 AMP).

The Spirit of Truth will reveal to us all truth, including things that have not even happened yet. I find what the *Jewish New Testament Commentary* has to say about this verse very interesting:

The Messianic life is lived by attentiveness to the Holy Spirit. Moreover, by telling His talmidim (disciples) that the Spirit of Truth will guide them into all truth and announce the events of the future, Yeshua virtually pre-authenticates the New Testament Scriptures, which they will write as a product of the Holy Spirit. He shows them that out of what He reveals to them will come the product of the Holy Spirit. We see that in Galatians, Ephesians, etc. In this mystery, He plans to reveal Himself in a greater dimension. Through

God's sovereignty, we can see how He reveals the timing of truth in relationship to the guidance and His revealing of the future.[1]

In the same way, Jesus lived in total unity with the Spirit of God and with the Father. We are also called to live completely dependent on the Spirit of God to reveal to us who God is and what God's actions will be. When we allow God the Holy Spirit to reveal to us what God is going to do, we can set our wills and actions in line with His will and actions. We can mimic Him in all things.

In order to live a "Messianic," or anointed life, as the Jewish Commentary says, we are required by God to allow His divine influence to flow perfectly through us, and to give it full access to every area of our being, thus shining forth the perfect image of the Father. Truly this is what it means to be anointed—to perfectly demonstrate God. A clear definition of anointing is, "God in man doing what man cannot do, but only God can do." The anointing is not self-willed or driven by soulical and inordinate desires; the anointing is God-willed, God-centered, and driven by God's power to produce God-results. If we do not set our mind on things above, thus rendering our own wills and desires dead, and our true life hidden with Christ in God, there is no way that the anointing can flow freely through us. If the pipe is clogged with dirt and garbage, the water cannot flow through it to quench our thirst.

People have made the question, "What would Jesus do?" a sort of generational slogan. If we really want to know what Jesus would do, we should look at what He said, not what we think about Him. Jesus said, "*My sustenance is to do the will of Him who sent Me, and to finish His work.*" Jesus was not interested in self-promotion. He knew that the only promotion that is worth anything in the eternal scheme of things is the promotion that comes from obedience to God; Jesus knew that God only promotes Himself. In order to rise to His full potential He had to deny Himself and go to the Cross.

What would Jesus do? He would do whatever He saw the Father doing. Emanuel, God with us, imitated His Father.

∽∽∽∽

God only promotes God.

∽∽∽∽

THE WORKING RELATIONSHIP

Do you know that even Jesus was subject to the sovereignty of God? It is true! I think sometimes we have a notion that Jesus was above God, or that He dictated to God; this could not be farther from the truth. Jesus was subject to God, because ***God only subjects Himself to Himself.*** It was completely natural for Jesus to be totally submitted to the Father, because for eternity, the Word had only moved forward when God the Father had spoken it. He never moved on His own; rather, He was released from the Father's mouth to accomplish the Father's will. In the same way, the God-breathed Word became the Living Word, a flesh-and-blood man, who was spoken forth out of the Father's mouth to realize the fullness of the Father's plan for His creation.

From the outstretched arm of eternity, the Word has always been eternally bound to the Father and to the Holy Spirit. They are in perfect unity of mind and purpose. They have but one will—that is, in and through all things, to bring to God the glory due His name. Jesus was thoroughly controlled by the Holy Spirit and totally submissive to God's timing in everything He did. When we read the story of Lazarus, we see that those too emotionally involved with the situation pleaded for Jesus to act more quickly than He did; yet Jesus waited for the perfect time in which God would receive the most glory.

> *Now a certain man was sick, Lazarus of Bethany, the town of Mary and her sister Martha. It was that Mary who anointed the Lord with fragrant oil and wiped His feet with her hair, whose brother Lazarus was sick. Therefore the sisters sent to Him, saying, "Lord, behold, he whom You love is sick." When Jesus heard that, He said, "This sickness is not unto death, but for the glory of God, that the Son of God may be glorified through it." ...So, when He heard that he was sick, He stayed two more days in the place where He was. ...So when Jesus came, He found that he had already been in the tomb four days. Now Bethany was near Jerusalem, about two miles away. ...Now Martha said to Jesus, "Lord, if You had been here, my brother would not have died. But even now I know that what-ever You ask of God, God will give You." Jesus said to her, "Your brother will rise again." Martha said to Him, "I know that he will rise again in the resurrection at the last day." Jesus said to her, "I am the resurrection and the life. He who believes in Me, though he may die, he shall live. And whoever lives and believes in Me shall never die. Do you believe this?" ...Then, when Mary came where Jesus was, and saw Him, she fell down at His feet, saying to Him, "Lord, if You had been here, my brother would not have died." Therefore, when Jesus saw her weeping, and the Jews who came with her weeping, He groaned in the spirit and was troubled* (John 11:1-4,6,17,21-26,32-33).

Jesus did not perform based on people's emotions, or whether or not they agreed with His actions. He was not interested in their opinion at all. His being was totally possessed by the Holy Spirit, and together, They perfectly carried out the will of God. Jesus was the God-man, His mind was the God-mind, and His will was the God-will. He carried out His identity as the Word of God become flesh with total confidence.

Likewise, we need to understand that the same anointed connection that binds the Father to the Son and to the Spirit, also is present within our very beings. God is bound to the Word in our hearts, to bring it to pass, and the Spirit is the one who accomplishes this process.

This divine relationship is not only manifesting in and through us so that the power of God will save us, set us free, and enable and equip our own lives. It has been given to us as a weapon to bring God's Kingdom to pass in other people's lives. In order to access and administer the outworkings of Christ, the power of the Anointed One's anointing, we must realize what the potential and purpose of God working with God is.

Remember that God said, "My people perish for lack of knowledge." The knowledge that the church needs in order to minister God's very nature and character to the nations is locked in the principles of God working with God. If we do not understand the working relationship between God and His Holy Spirit, we will miss out on the lifestyle of being led by the Holy Spirit in every situation. It is His Spirit that reminds us of the promises of His Word. It is His Spirit that indwells us, enduing us with power from on high, anointing us to destroy strongholds and defeat the spiritual principalities of darkness; and it is His Spirit that is able to defeat every enemy using His greatest weapon—the Word of God.

The two are intricately tied together; they are inseparable. It is the Holy Spirit that leads us into the very presence of God, making the Word become flesh in our lives so that God can become one with Himself. If we deny the power of His Spirit, or somehow miss the importance of the working relationship within the Godhead, we will miss the opportunity to be led moment by moment further into the

presence of a holy and matchless God. By undermining this powerful relationship, we will miss what is available to us through the Holy
Spirit: God's 24-hour, tangible, abiding presence and divine influence. The outcome of knowledge will be the flow of the supernatural through our lives, manifesting in miracles, signs, and wonders.

We know that Jesus studied the Scriptures as a child. This was a
normal behavior for Jewish boys from all kinds of backgrounds and
families; the Torah was the place from which the Jews gained their
identity. They bound it to their foreheads and wrists and embroi-
dered it on their clothing. They wrote it on the doorposts and lintels
of their houses. On a side note, is it not interesting that the blood of
the lamb was also placed on the doorposts and lintels of the Hebrew
homes in the land of Goshen, so that when the angel of death came
to take the firstborn, it did not touch them?

The Blood of the Lamb and the Word of God are one and the
same, our protection, and our security against death; for by it we
have overcome sin, hell, death, and the grave! It is by the Blood of
the Lamb and the Word of our Testimony (the Word of the New
Covenant through Jesus Christ) that we have become overcomers.

When Jesus was led by the Holy Spirit into the wilderness to be
tempted by the devil, how did Jesus answer His accuser? Yes, it was
with the Scripture. It is very intriguing to me that the Holy Spirit *led*
Jesus into the desert to be tempted. God wanted the Word that was
in Jesus to be tested and proven to be correct. Jesus had to rely on
the Holy Spirit to bring it to His remembrance, just as we also do. It
was only after Jesus was filled with the Holy Spirit and the Father
spoke from Heaven, saying, *"This is My Beloved Son, in whom I am
well pleased,"* that Jesus underwent severe testing.

After studying the Word as a boy, and discovering His true identity as the Messiah within its words, His Father in Heaven confirmed His calling, and He was anointed by the Holy Spirit to fulfill
the call of God on His life. This is the same process that we should

be experiencing in our own lives. God is the One who calls us to His power; yet just as John the Baptist was sent to be a witness to Jesus' anointing, and just as God the Father spoke with an audible voice, confirming His Son, so we will also be recognized and confirmed by the spiritual leaders in our lives.

God has given us spiritual leaders to confirm us, train us, and discipline us in the call of God and the supernatural flow of the anointing. Remember, Jesus did no mighty signs and wonders before He was recognized by His Father God and was anointed by the Holy Spirit with power from on high. In all of these circumstances and signs, we see the working relationship between the Father, the Son, and the Holy Spirit.

Another interesting fact is that Jesus fasted of His own volition, not because He was commanded to by the Holy Spirit. It was the Holy Spirit who led Him into the wilderness, but it was the Word of God within Him that spoke to Him to fast for 40 days. He had probably meditated hours and hours upon the stories of Moses and his experience on Mount Sinai. Jesus could see in the spirit that He was going through the same ordeal, and He knew from the Word what would be required of Him as the second Moses.

> *Then Jesus, being filled with the Holy Spirit, returned from the Jordan and was led by the Spirit into the wilderness, being tempted for forty days by the devil. And in those days He ate nothing, and afterward, when they had ended, He was hungry* (Luke 4:1-2).

There is a powerful revelation locked up in the next few verses, where Jesus' responses to the devil's temptations are recorded. Jesus speaks the Word of God out loud, therefore silencing the lies of the enemy. How is that possible? Simply put, a *God who does not speak is no God at all.* Jesus gives God voice. If God had not spoken, there would have been no creation, no universe, for the breath of God makes galaxies of stars come into being. Honestly, God does not even have to speak for things to be shaken up. He merely has to huff some air out of His nostrils and all His enemies are scattered! If that kind of power is contained merely within His breath, it should definitely stir us up to rely on the power of His Word.

The truth is that Jesus will always speak God forth. When Christ is truly operating through a person, the Word of God will be flowing out of that person's mouth. The Scripture teaches us that God does not do anything unless He first reveals it to the men who have sought His face:

> *I have also spoken by the prophets, and have multiplied visions; I have given symbols through the witness of the prophets* (Hosea 12:10).

> *Surely the Lord God does nothing, unless He reveals His secret to His servants the prophets. A lion has roared! Who will not fear? The Lord God has spoken! Who can but prophesy?* (Amos 3:7-8).

God is adamant about using men and women of faith to speak forth His Word. His desire to produce Himself is so great that He is willing to allow His massive, earth-splitting voice that shakes both heaven and earth to be released through the tongues of people who have yielded themselves to Him. Of course, God can speak on His own. He is not in need of human voices. However, because He has bound Himself by covenantal relationship to mankind, He is bound by His own Word to produce His nature and character in and through man. This divine reproduction can only occur as God in Heaven becomes intimately bound to the God-seed of His Word inside of His children. As the Holy Spirit hovers over the Word, its power will become alive inside of you, giving to you and releasing through you the ability to reshape and mold your world until it takes on the perfect appearance of God's Word.

Let us look at Jesus' responses to the devil's weak and meagerly attempts to catch Him.

> *And the devil said to Him, "If You are the Son of God, command this stone to become bread." But Jesus answered him, saying, "It is written, 'Man shall not live by bread alone, but by every word of God.'" Then the devil, taking Him up on a high mountain, showed Him all the kingdoms of the world in a moment of time. And the devil said to Him, "All this authority I will give You, and their glory; for this has been delivered to me, and I give it to whomever I wish. Therefore, if You will worship before me, all will be Yours." And Jesus answered and said to him, "Get behind Me, Satan! For it is written, 'You shall worship the Lord your God, and Him only you shall serve'"* (Luke 4:3-8).

Jesus knew there was but one weapon that the Holy Spirit would wield against the enemy in order to defeat him; only one sharp, two-edged sword that always silences the attacks of the wicked one. Satan cannot answer back to the Word except with deception. He will attempt to blind your eyes from seeing in the realms of the spirit, to see that he is already defeated. The devil's hope is that He can keep you from truly seeing that he really is a slave to his own failure. Satan did not know that by tempting Jesus, he would actually stir up the Word and the Spirit within Jesus, so that He was empowered to fulfill God's Word in the earth.

One tool that satan uses against the children of God is ignorance. Do you know that he thrives on ignorance? Satan is attracted to it and works with it to manipulate and twist the truth of God's Word. When a person is ignorant of what God says about a certain situation, it is a very simple thing for the devil to speak lies to that person because they have not been trained to know the difference between truth and a lie. As long as a person refuses to partake of God's Word, their growth will be stunted, their eyes will be blind, and their ears will be deaf; only the Word of God gives sight to the blind, and hearing to the deaf. Only God's Word can raise the dead and cast out the devils; and it is only through God's Word that we can discover who Christ is and who we are in Christ.

Jesus did not have to think about how He would respond to the mockery of the devil. He did not have to run to the synagogue to read the scrolls quickly to see what God had to say about satan's taunting. No, He had memorized the Word of God, had it written on His heart and mind. When the devil spoke to Jesus from his own resource of lies, Jesus spoke from His resource of truth: the Word.

Then Jesus returned in the power of the Spirit to Galilee, and news of Him went out through all the surrounding region (Luke 4:14).

Many people do not realize that Jesus never performed any miracles or signs and wonders until He came out of the wilderness in the power of the Spirit. The purpose of His 40-day excursion to the desert was to totally sacrifice all of His humanity to the working relationship between God the Father, the Word, and the Spirit. If He had never been tested, where would His confidence have lain? Where would His dependence on the Word and the Spirit be?

It was imperative that Jesus truly understand who He was, who God was in Him, and how the Spirit of God was working with the Word in Him. In the same way, before mighty miracles can take place in our lives we have to recognize that Christ in us is the source of God flowing out of us. As we yield to the Spirit and feed our spirits with the Word, we will be able to overcome every obstacle that the devil puts before our feet to make us stumble.

And He was handed the book of the prophet Isaiah. And when He had opened the book, He found the place where it was written: "The Spirit of the Lord is upon Me… (Luke 4:17-18a).

This verse makes it clear that Jesus is claiming to be anointed as King. There is no difference between His claim to the throne and David's or Solomon's, who also claimed to be anointed as king. When the prophet Samuel went to the city of Bethlehem in First Kings, God said that he would be shown who among the sons of Jesse had been chosen as king. When David came into the room, the Lord said, "Rise, Samuel, and anoint him. For I have chosen him to be king over My people Israel." As Samuel broke the horn of anointing oil over David's head, the prophet was proclaiming to everyone that this is whom God has chosen; he is the rightful king of Israel. David's right to rule did not come from the people of Israel recognizing who he was. God, not the people, had given him that position. Their only job was to correctly discern who he was and the anointing on his life, so that they could submit to him as God's chosen.

In the same way Jesus is saying, "Whether you have eyes to see or not, I have been anointed by the Father as King of kings and Lord of lords. You did not choose Me; God did, and He has confirmed it by sending the anointing of His Holy Spirit upon Me." Jesus is Lord over everything that exists, both in Heaven and on earth. Even those things, which in outward appearance seem not to be of God, or oppose God in any way, are also under His Lordship. The Scripture does not teach us that His authority and dominion are somehow limited by sin. No; He is the Sovereign Ruler over all things, and to His mighty name every knee shall bow and every tongue shall take an oath; there is coming a day when all will recognize Christ Jesus our Lord and confess that He is God.

The Spirit of the Lord is upon Me, because He has anointed Me to preach the gospel to the poor; He has sent Me to heal the brokenhearted, to proclaim liberty to the captives and recovery of sight to the blind, to set at liberty those who are oppressed (Luke 4:18).

As I mentioned before, Jesus had tested these words and found them to be true in the wilderness. He had meditated on them both night and day, until they were deeply ingrained on His mind. He had considered them and pondered them and believed them, until God's timing made them a reality. When these words came to pass in Jesus' life, a stunning thing occurred: signs, wonders, and miracles were birthed in the natural from God's Word becoming reality in the natural.

Everything that God has said is already accomplished in the spirit realms (for He says of Himself, I am, and I will never change; I am the same yesterday, today, and forever. I am the self-existent One). In other words, God is already fully consummate; His perfection is not bound by time, and neither is His Word, for they are one. Yet, in the natural, in this time realm, God is releasing certain aspects of His Word into the earth at certain times.

In like manner, God wants to accomplish His Word in us, thus releasing His power to destroy the works of the devil and set people free from every kind of sickness and bondage. As we meditate on God's Word, we will see that the more we yield to the glory contained in His Word, the more we will see signs and wonders brought to pass through us; His Word will become flesh and we will behold His glory, full of grace and truth.

I have heard many people say, "I am filled with the Holy Spirit," or "I received the Holy Spirit," or "I have the Holy Spirit." Yet, it is one thing to say we possess the Baptizer; it is a completely different thing to be possessed by the Baptizer! When we first become a

Christian, we cry out and say, "Jesus, You are my Lord!" If this is true, then the Lord ought to come and possess His property.

The culture in which Jesus lived was one of kings, lords, servants, and slaves. If a man was the lord of a certain area of land, anyone living within the boundaries of his property was now his to do with as he willed. They were his slaves and were totally dependent on him for survival. In the same way, when kings and lords would go out to have combat with other nations, whatever land they captured from their enemy became theirs; they possessed it and everything in it was procured for personal benefit.

When we cry out to Jesus, "You are my Lord," we should expect that Jesus will come and possess what belongs to Him. If He has not come and possessed us, then it is obvious He is not truly our Lord. God is interested in His children being totally saturated with His Word, completely possessed by Him, so that our minds are captive to God and our tongues are controlled by His nature and character. His desire is to train us to release Christ through our words, just as He does. Out of the abundance of the heart, the mouth speaks.

Maybe we should consider the conversations we have had over the past week. Were they birthed out of the Word or were they a mixture of God and the flesh? A mixture between God and self will never produce anything but lukewarm Christians without any real power. But if God possesses us, the purity of His Word will produce purity and power in other people, as well as our own lives. Our words are a window into our hearts. Every time we speak, we give people a look at what is inside of us. Words determine our future path. They can attract people or repel them. They reveal to us how much of God is already at work on the inside, as well as showing us the strength of the miraculous in our lives.

MYSTERIES: THE WORK OF GOD INSIDE

I have had many interesting experiences while reading the Word of God. One time I was sitting peacefully in my office reading from the Book of Ephesians. The presence of the Holy Spirit was so strong that day, and as I read I could feel the Spirit resting upon the Word, taking delight in it as I sustained my spirit with God's manna. I kept feeling as if the Spirit was telling me what He was going to say next. I wanted to test my ability to really hear and respond to both the Word and the Holy Spirit. I read to the end of the page. Immediately I ran upstairs and told my wife to turn the page. As she did, I spoke what I felt the Holy Spirit was saying, and without the help of memorization of the next few verses, I declared to her exactly what the next few verses said! By merely allowing the Spirit to work with the Word, I was able to tap into the supernatural flow that originally caused those words to be written down.

In one sense, this is how we receive the *rhema* Word of God. There is a distinction made between the written word, or *logos* in the Greek, and a prophetic word directly for a specific circumstance that comes out of the written word, which is the definition of rhema. Rhema is birthed when the written logos takes on voice in a person's life. Rhema is the product of the Spirit of God resting on the Word of God; the Holy Spirit brings forth revelation that when spoken out, sets many free and lifts them to a higher realm of understanding in Christ. By allowing the logos to become rhema in our own lives, we will be enabled to declare and unveil the mysteries of God and His Word. The Scriptures tell us that even the principalities and powers in heavenly places are waiting for us to make known to them the mysteries of God!

And to make all see what is the fellowship of the mystery, which from the beginning of the ages has been hidden in God who created all things through Jesus Christ; to the intent that now the manifold wisdom of God might be made known by the church to the principalities and powers in the heavenly places, according to the eternal purpose which He accomplished in Christ Jesus our Lord, in whom we have boldness and access with confidence through faith in Him (Ephesians 3:9-12).

The Book of Ephesians mentions this word "mystery" very often, so I want to specifically look at its meaning in the Greek. According to the *New Strong's Expanded Exhaustive Concordance of the Bible,* the word that we translate "mystery" in English is the word *musterion,* which means, "to shut the mouth; a secret or 'mystery,' through the idea of silence imposed by initiation into religious rites. Musterion in the New Testament denotes, not the mysterious (as with the English word), but that which being outside the range of unassisted natural apprehension, can be made known only by divine revelation, and is made known in a manner and at a time appointed by God, and to those only who are illuminated by His Spirit...."[2] The way that we usually use this word, it connotes information that not everyone, or in some cases, no one is a partaker of. Interestingly enough, the Scriptural use of this word actually paints a picture of the opposite. Paul makes it very clear that the Spirit of God who searches the deep things of God is unveiling the mysteries of Christ.

At this time in history, there was a strong movement to return to the teachings and natural wisdom of Aristotle and Plato, who had been part of a secret society, who prided themselves on the hidden wisdom that they had discovered. These scholars and teachers seemed to know things about nature and human beings that the common people did not know; they guarded it and treasured it, even above human relationships. During the time of Paul's life, there was also a group of people who had formed after the death of Christ who held to a doctrine called Gnosticism. This cult denounced that Jesus came as a physical man because they believed the body was evil. Also among their beliefs was the idea that there are hidden mysteries in the Word, or about Jesus in general, that would only be revealed to a few, very special people. Paul very clearly is attacking this doctrine in His writings to the Ephesians. The apostle wants to open our eyes to the fact that God desires to unveil the truth to us so that we can have access to His very mind.

It is obvious that the wisdom and knowledge that we have unlimited access to through the Holy Spirit is far superior to the limited human understanding that Aristotle and Plato were familiar with. These mysteries, which find their birthplace in the heart of God, have in actuality been planted deep within us, so that we no longer have to grasp and beg to be exposed to God's thoughts and creativity. Once a child has been given the thing for which he was whining he should stop asking for it, correct? His need has been met; his desire has been fulfilled. He no longer has to beg for the thing, because it is in his hands.

It would be utterly ridiculous for me, if after having received something from a friend or my family, to throw it down, turn my hands toward heaven, and begin shouting for it again. It is the same way with the mysteries of God. Paul teaches us that we have the right and privilege to come boldly into God's presence and access the secrets of the universe, which He has laid up for us there. Again, this shows us the importance of praying in the Spirit, because, as Paul says in First Corinthians 14, when we pray in the spirit we are speaking mysteries to the Father. This is clearly the method, sign, and wonder that God has chosen to use to speak to His people. Isaiah 28:11 says, "*With stammering lips and another tongue* [God] *will speak to* [His] *people.*" God wants to reveal Himself through mysteries, so that His Spirit inside of us can go to work with those mysteries and reveal God's nature and character through us.

For this reason I, Paul, the prisoner of Christ Jesus for you Gentiles—if indeed you have heard of the dispensation of the grace of God which was given to me for you, how that by

revelation He made known to me the mystery (as I have
briefly written already, by which, when you read, you may
understand my knowledge in the mystery of Christ)
(Ephesians 3:1-4).

When I read this verse, I clearly understand and know that there
is nothing I can share concerning the mysteries of God that did not
come by grace. The truth is that just as God spoke through the apostle Paul, God is working with His Word speaking through us.
Whatever power and authority was available to the first apostles and
prophets and the people who followed them, is also available to us
today.

In the New Testament we see how God raised up mighty apostles, and as time went on we see how those who were obedient to the
faith, full of the Holy Spirit and power, began to experience the flow
of the anointing that came through God's apostolic authority as they
were being trained in the Word and the Spirit. They became empowered by the Holy Spirit and did mighty signs and wonders.

If we say that these men who wrote the Scriptures are the only
ones who were able to reach and understand the mysteries of God,
how then is it possible that Stephen and Philip, who were both called
to serve tables at the beginning, did mighty signs and wonders, healing the sick and raising the dead? No, my friends, God's power is not
for "the elite." It is for every believer who will choose to yield to
God's Word.

Paul's experience of being caught up into the third heaven and
seeing amazing things, which cannot be uttered, was actually the
birthplace for the revelation that Paul had about Christ. It was in the
throne room that God downloaded His own thoughts into Paul's
head so that Paul would be able to receive the mysteries of Christ.
Paul learned to minister God's secrets from the throne room. That is
why he said to the Colossians, "Set your minds on things above, not

on things of the earth." In essence, Paul is saying, do not try to understand the things of God from an earthly and natural perspective; it won't work! We have to learn to tap into God's mind in order to understand the deep things of God.

Early on in my ministry, I had a very similar experience to Paul's. During a time of strong prayer, I had the sensation that I was no longer in the room where I was praying. When I opened my eyes, I was in the throne room of God. The room was full of an indescribable light, which filled every corner of its immense space. In the center of the room there was an object from which all of the brilliant light was emanating. The focal point of every activity and movement in the room was centered on the glowing, radiant, light-creating throne of God; and out of the throne I saw the hand of God moving.

Suddenly, I saw a form come out of the throne. It was only after He moved farther away from the throne that I could tell it was Jesus. Whenever Jesus would come close to the throne, it was as if the throne would swallow Him up—the two would become one. When He stepped out from the throne, I could see Jesus in His humanity: I saw the scars in His wrists from where He was nailed to the Cross. I could see that He was still a man with a body and all the features of a man. Yet when He entered into the throne, I could not discern a difference between Him and the Father. He was who He really is, and that is one with the Father.

This vision can only be explained through Scripture.

Which in other ages was not made known to the sons of men, as it has now been revealed by the Spirit to His holy apostles and prophets.... To me, who am less than the least of all the saints, this grace was given, that I should preach among the Gentiles the unsearchable riches of Christ (Ephesians 3:5,8).

WHAT IS THE MYSTERY?

The mystery of who God is, is wrapped up in the revelation of God working with God. When we fully grasp that it is God in Heaven working with God in us, we will see that the mystery of God's will, the supernatural flow of His Holy Spirit, and the power of His Word all work intimately together to cause an explosion of God within our lives, and the amazing outworkings of His Godhead through us. The working relationship between the Father, the Son, and the Holy Spirit cuts to the very heart of the issue of who Christ really is and who He can be in us. We have to know that everything Jesus claimed to be, that He truly is. He has never told a lie, nor was any deceit found in Him.

We need to dive deep into the revelation of who Christ is so that we can tap into who we are. As we can see from Colossians, God has no desire to keep it a secret, nor to hide Himself from us.

To them God willed to make known what are the riches of the glory of this mystery among the Gentiles: which is Christ in you, the hope of glory. Him we preach, warning every man and teaching every man in all wisdom, that we may present every man perfect in Christ Jesus (Colossians 1:27-28).

I realize that the Old Covenant tabernacle no longer exists, nor does Solomon's temple; but I do know this: if they did, God would not be there! The glory no longer dwells in buildings made by man's hands. The glory has come to the new tabernacle within us! Our bodies are now the temples of the Holy Spirit. God, in His sovereignty, chose us to be vessels of honor and glory before Him forever, and has poured out the riches of His glory upon us without measure. We have this treasure in earthen vessels that the Excellency may be of God and not of man.

Within the realms of praise, God shows us once again that He works with Himself. The Scripture teaches that God inhabits the praises of His people. God is drawn to love and adoration because they are a very important part of His nature and character. When we release love to God, He is going to come and possess us, not just by dwelling among us, but much greater than that, living in and through us.

When the women who had served Jesus came to the tomb on the first day of the week, they encountered two angels, one standing at the foot of the bed on which Jesus was laid, and one standing at the head. They looked at the women and said, "We know whom you seek: Jesus of Nazareth. He is not here! He is risen!" This picture is symbolic of the Ark of the Covenant, which held the tablets of the law, the manna, which had come from Heaven, and Aaron's rod that had budded. On the top of the ark, there were two angels, cherubim, who covered the mercy seat with their wings. "The glory of God no longer rests above the mercy seat," the angels were telling the women. "He has risen and the glory of the Lord now dwells in you!"

In Christ dwells the fullness of the Godhead bodily, and Christ in us is the hope of glory. In other words, all of the fullness of the Godhead bodily within us is going to cause God's glory to fill the earth as the waters cover the sea (see Isa. 60).

Remember what the word "Christ" really means. *Christ* is the Greek word for Messiah, or anointed one. Right now we have the Anointed One's anointing dwelling inside of us and working through us. It is the anointing within us that is responsible for producing the true manifestation of the Word of God. The anointing within you is responsible for bringing into place the incarnate nature of Christ.

Note how *The International Standard Bible Encyclopedia* characterizes the powerful revelation of Christ toward us:

Jesus is all that God is, and He alone is this. Of this "only begotten God" it is now declared that He "is"—not "was," the state is not one which has been left behind at the incarnation, but one which continues uninterrupted and unmodified—"into"—not merely "in"—"the bosom of the Father"—that is to say, He continues in the most intimate and complete communion with the Father. Though now incarnate, He is still "with God" in the full sense of the external relation intimated in John 1:1. This being true, He has much more than seen God, and is fully able to "interpret" God to men. Though no one has ever yet seen God, yet he who has seen Jesus Christ, "God's only begotten," has seen the Father. In this remarkable sentence there is asserted in the most direct manner the full Deity of the incarnate Word, and the continuity of His life as such in His incarnate life; thus He is fitted to be the absolute revelation of God to man.[3]

The anointing creates a responsibility to catalyze God's creativity, just as the perfect man Adam was a catalyst for God's perfect destiny to be released into His world. This is our calling: to fully allow the manifestation of God to rule and reign in us as kings and priests forever after the order of Melchizedek.

Christ in you is the hope of glory. In other words, Christ in you is responsible for bringing forth this manifestation of the Word. When the Word becomes flesh, we behold His glory, full of grace and truth. God's glory is the end result of the Word becoming flesh. We see the authority of God's omnipotence, omniscience, and omnipresence having its creative rule and reign and full manifestation in those yielded to the Father through the agreement of His Word and Spirit.

This was not only Jesus' destiny, but it is also ours. We are called to be the perfect image of the Father, upholding all things by the

Word of His power. Let us look at another verse that confirms to us that we are to be carriers of God's revealed secrets, unveiling our faces so that the glory of the Gospel of Jesus Christ, which shines forth from us, can be fully seen by those who are currently serving the god of this world.

> *Let a man so consider us, as servants of Christ and stewards of the mysteries of God* (1 Corinthians 4:1).

As children of God, we should have an earnest expectation that the Messiah's anointing and the mystery of God's will are going to flow through us freely whenever we are called to minister. When I step behind the pulpit with holy utterance to speak into hundreds of lives, I have confidence that the Spirit of God is upon me and God's Word is in my mouth. All of the knowledge that is within me comes from the unlimited source of knowledge in the Holy Spirit. All I am is a conduit empowered by the love of God for that wisdom and knowledge to come out of. I have boldness toward men and God that the Holy Spirit within me is going to work with the Word of God within me to produce God's results. The Spirit is going to take up His weapon of choice and utterly obliterate the plans and devices of the enemy. Christ in me, which is the hope of glory, directed by the Holy Spirit, will take my words, which are God's and cut into the heart of every person listening to plant God inside of them; and so the working relationship between God the Spirit and God the Word will be sown into other people's lives.

CONCLUSION

I realize that we have covered an immense amount of information within this chapter, but I want you to know: You have the mind of Christ, and you can receive the things of the Spirit. Remember, it is God who called you, therefore it will be God in Heaven working with God within you who will accomplish God's perfect will. All you have to do is yield to His Word, and then watch God's nature and character take on wings in your life. Let's go over a few of the key points from Chapter Five.

One of Jesus' favorite ways to instruct the multitude was by speaking to them in parables. The reason He did this was to bypass their emotions and mind, and speak straight to their spirit. Jesus wanted to plant a seed of God within them, and He did not want that seed to be uprooted by the flesh. The same is true with His disciples. Jesus was not interested in speaking to their emotions. He wanted them to grasp hold of the Word of God and not be afraid to believe it. When we come into close intimate relationship with God, where He can begin to train us, God will use parables in our lives to plant a seed of His nature and character within us, thereby giving the Holy Spirit a God-seed to work with, and completely bypassing the flesh.

Another important principle we discussed in this chapter is how the God-working-with-God relationship within us will unveil the mysteries of God to us. God's mysteries are not only for the elite, the well-educated, or the wealthy, though all of these people can also be partakers of His secrets. The mystery of the riches of Christ are for those who choose to yield themselves to God's sovereign will for their lives—which is His Word. When we allow His Word to be planted in our hearts, when we allow the Spirit of God to work with that Word, God Himself will explode within us, until He is living and breathing, ruling and reigning through us.

The power of God working with God is in the working relationship between the Father, the Son, and the Holy Spirit, which is so evident to us when we study the life of Jesus Christ. The Word became flesh and dwelt among us; we have beheld His glory, full of grace and truth. The Word was made perfect through suffering, states the author of the Book of Hebrews, and was acquainted with the tactics and temptations that all men face; and yet, He was without sin. How did He overcome, you ask? It was because He yielded Himself to the God-working-with-God relationship that He was born to manifest.

Our destiny is to show forth the glory of the Son in the same fashion and brilliance that He did. In fact, He has called us to do even greater works than He did on the earth, because He has gone to be with His Father. The perfect relationship, which is present in Heaven right now and is continually producing more of God's nature and character, is destined to be achieved in our everyday living.

TIMELESS TRUTHS FROM CHAPTER FIVE

- If we place a high value in God's Word, reverencing and respecting it, we can have an expectation to encounter God; for God and His Word are one.

- Anytime you walk out the nature of God, you silence spiritual warfare.

- When truth takes on wings, you will discover total freedom.

- Parables are mysteries intended for revelation through relationship and discipleship.

- First you must know the truth, then the One Jesus who is the Truth, the Way, and the Life will set truth free.

- Truth only sets truth free in the same way God only sets God free.

- When a person's soul or flesh speaks louder than their spirit, you will have a check; but when their spirit speaks louder than their soul or flesh, you will have peace.

- It is only God in intimate contact with God that will produce what is of God.

- Draw near to God; He will draw near to you.

ENDNOTES

1. David H. Stern, *Jewish New Testament Commentary* (Clarksville, MD: Jewish New Testament Publications, 1992), 202.

2. James Strong, *The New Strong's Expanded Exhaustive Concordance of the Bible: The New Strong's Expanded Dictionary of the Words in the Greek New Testament* (Nashville, TN: Thomas Nelson Publishers, 2001), 168.

3. James Orr, ed., "Person of Christ, 4-5," *International Standard Bible Encyclopedia*, accessed on the Internet at: http://www.searchgodsword.org/enc/isb/view.cgi?number=T6826.

CONCLUSION

We've Only Just Begun

Mercy and truth have met together; righteousness and peace have kissed. Truth shall spring out of the earth, and righteousness shall look down from heaven (Psalm 85:10-11).

IMAGINE that you are driving down the road and someone cuts you off. You have two options: Stay in peace and release longsuffering, gentleness, and patience, or get angry, possibly curse, and be frustrated. With either response we will see the God-working-with-God principle in action along with the Law of Reciprocity. At the very beginning of this book, we learned how the thoughts and ideas you send out about a person are either going to attract God or attract satan; because God works with God, and satan works with satan.

Let's say you take the first response. From what we have discussed, that would be to release the nature of God thus attracting God. This decision activates the fruit of the Spirit, which is the nature of God, and you attract the spirit of intercession. Immediately God goes to work with God and you start praying for that person's safety.

The second response (get angry, possibly curse, and be frustrated) would attract the nature of satan—in the same way as when King Saul got angry and it attracted evil spirits. This is a simplistic way of looking at the God-working-with-God principle and the Law of Reciprocity. If we choose to release God's love, we will attract more of God's love to us. If we speak God's Word, the Spirit will go to work with the Word, thus producing more of God in and through us.

Let's review again the Law of Reciprocity:

- Forgive and it will be forgiven you.

- If you don't forgive, it won't be forgiven.

- Give and it will be given to you.

- God loves those who love (God) Him.

- If you show mercy, you will reap mercy.

- God is righteous; He loves the righteous.

- Honor God and He will honor you.

- You shall know the truth. Truth sets truth free.

- To whom much is given, much is required.

- Draw near to God and He will draw near to you.

The mighty revelation of *God working with God* is one that stretches from before the foundations of the earth to the end of time and beyond. In this first volume we have only begun to touch on this fantastic resource for understanding God's limitless power, glory, and love. We have only just begun to tap into the principle of God working with God!

I invite you to check out the other books in this series, as well as my other writings, for further study. May God bless you!

REFERENCES

Gesenius, H.W.F. *Gesenius' Hebrew-Chaldee Lexicon to the Old Testament*. Grand Rapids, MI: Baker Book House Company, 1970.

Munroe, Myles. *Releasing Your Potential*. Shippensburg, PA: Destiny Image Publishers, 1992.

Stern, David H. *Jewish New Testament Commentary*. Clarksville, MD: Jewish New Testament Publications, 1992.

Strong, James. *The New Strong's Expanded Exhaustive Concordance of the Bible: Strong's Expanded Dictionary of the Words in the Hebrew Bible*. Nashville, TN: Thomas Nelson Publishers, 2001.

Strong, James. *The New Strong's Expanded Exhaustive Concordance of the Bible: The New Strong's Expanded Dictionary of the Words in the Greek New Testament*. Nashville, TN: Thomas Nelson Publishers, 2001.

Wheeler, Douglas A. *For the Love of God: A Conceptual Study of the Love of God*. Bossier City, LA: Mended Wing Ministries, 1996.

MINISTRY RESOURCES

Would you like to access more life-changing resources concerning *God Working With God* and the *Law of Reciprocity*? They are available at your convenience at the Sword Ministries International Website: www.swordministries.org. On this exciting Website, not only will you learn more about *God Working With God*, but you will also be tapping into an unlimited well of God's supernatural wisdom concerning all areas of life and ministry.

Apostolic Revivalist Warren Hunter has authored over 18 books, full of God's power and presence, which will aid you in drawing near to the Father. Also, you can hear firsthand about the awesome move of God that is being birthed by the Holy Spirit through the Holy Spirit. Learn about the amazing miracles that are taking place all over the world with just a click of your mouse!

In addition to this first volume, Apostolic Revivalist Warren Hunter is in the process of publishing other important *God Working With God (GWWG)* volumes, including:

GWWG: Love & Worship

GWWG: Faith

GWWG: God in Your Mouth

GWWG: Spirit to Spirit

GWWG: God Hears Himself

Many others will be coming your way very soon as well! These books cover a multitude of subjects, such as prayer, intimacy with God, exercising the God kind of faith, and others. Look for them in bookstores soon, and remember: God in you is working with God!

Author's Contact Information

Sword Ministries
P.O. Box 7360
Branson, MO 65615

BECOME A CARRIER OF REVIVAL!

God wants you to preach His Gospel with the **power** and **demonstration of the Holy Spirit**. Join Apostolic Revivalist Warren Hunter in "Supernatural Leadership Training Institute: School of the Revivalist!"

Apostolic Revivalist Warren Hunter will train you, through **21 DVD training sessions**, to minister in the power of the Holy Spirit with signs and wonders following. Included with the 21 DVD set is the **School of the Revivalist Training Manual**.

Within the training manual are **outlines for each DVD as well as 21 outworking assignments**. This school is not designed for the Sunday pew sitter. After you complete the 21 DVDs and the assignments, you will be ministering in the power of God to your friends, family, and community!

License and ordination are available upon meeting predetermined requirements. Order now for **$495.00** by calling **417-335-7650** or going to www.swordministries.org.

Additional copies of this book and other
book titles from DESTINY IMAGE are
available at your local bookstore.

Call toll free: 1-800-722-6774.

Send a request for a catalog to:

Destiny Image® Publishers, Inc.
P.O. Box 310
Shippensburg, PA 17257-0310

*"Speaking to the Purposes of God for this
Generation and for the Generations to Come."*

For a complete list of our titles,
visit us at www.destinyimage.com